The Cooler's Grimoire

The Comprehensive Instructional
Guide to Nightclub & Bar Security

Ivan 'Doc' Holiday

Outskirts Press Inc

Denver, Colorado

The Cooler's Grimoire
The Comprehensive Instructional Guide to Nightclub & Bar Security
All Rights Reserved.
Copyright © 2008 Ivan 'Doc' Holiday
V2.0

Outskirts Press, Inc.
http://www.outskirtspress.com

ISBN: 978-1-4327-2641-6

Outskirts Press and the "OP" logo are trademarks belonging to Outskirts Press, Inc.

PRINTED IN THE UNITED STATES OF AMERICA

In Memory of
Imette St. Guillen

Injustice anywhere is a threat to justice everywhere. We are caught in an inescapable network of mutuality, tied in a single garment of destiny. Whatever affects one directly, affects all indirectly.

Martin Luther King Jr.

About the Author

Ivan 'Doc' Holiday

Ivan Holiday Arsenault was born in New Brunswick, Canada. Received an honorable discharge from the Canadian Armed Forces in 1980.
In 1981 joined Burns Security and worked as personal security to the French Ambassador to Canada in Edmonton, Alberta Canada.
In 1982 Ivan worked his first bouncing job at the Forum Inn in Edmonton, Alberta. At 50 years old, Ivan "Doc" Holiday has worked a total of 53 nightclubs and bars over a period of 26 years. He is recognized worldwide as a leading authority in the field of nightclub security. Ivan is the author of the book "The Bouncer's Bible – The Art and Science of working the door."

In 1999 he produced the World's First and only Nightclub Security Instructional Video/DVD under the same title.

Ivan is founder and president of BouncerGear Inc. He is a registered Bodyguard with SEAL Bodyguard International, Canadian Government file # TN57496 and a member of Blackwater Worldwide file # F0B0502. Ivan has both his Florida 'D' class and armed 'G' class security certifications. Ivan is a certified instructor of MEB tactical Baton and OCAT Pepper Spray. While working as a bouncer, Ivan attained an AS degree in Computer Science from McKay College in 1985. In 1986 Ivan invented The CRV -Child's Riding Belt a device that allowed children to ride safely with an adult on Motorcycles, ATV's, Snowmobiles..etc. Later Ivan was nominated for an Honorary Ph.D. from the University of Alberta Canada, in recognition of his creation of the CRV Riding Belt and its contribution toward the rehabilitation of paraplegic children. In 1993 sponsored by Castrol Canada & Alberta Cycle, Ivan won the Western Canadian Am. Superbike Championship in Calgary, Alberta, Canada. Over a period of 9 years Ivan continued to educate himself via internet studies, attending classes, workshops, seminars and lectures. Ivan earned his BA in Criminology from Concordia University, MA in Ancient Western Philosophy and a Ph.D. in Psychology from Stanford Hill University. Ivan researched a 22,444 word-110 page Doctorate Thesis titled "The Psychological Profile of Serial Homicide" to attain his Ph.D. Major in Correctional Psychology. In 2003-2004 Ivan completed a two-year Internship at the Hastings Youth Academy with the Florida Dept. of Juvenile Justice working as an intern psychologist. He was employed as an Adjunct Psychology Professor teaching undergraduate psychology at Bethune-Cookman College.

Ivan wrote and passed the National Clinical Mental Health Counselor Exam at the University of Florida in the spring of 2005.

Ivan worked as a Correctional Psychologist with the Florida Dept. of Corrections at the UCI- Level 7 Maximum Security prison until October of 2005. A Member in good standing with the Florida Peace Officers Association, Ivan was Top Marksman on the 2005 UCI Combat Pistol team. Ivan was a Gold medal winner at the RMC Invitational Pistol Match. In June 2007, Ivan qualified for his 'G' class armed security license and concealed weapons permit with a written score of 92% and a shooting score of 214 out of 218.

Ivan is a MENSA America member with a WAIS-III I.Q. score of 144.

On April 10, 2008 Ivan opened the Bouncergear Inc Nightclub Security Academy in Daytona Beach, Florida.

WWW.BOUNCERGEARCORP.COM

WWW.BOUNCERSBIBLE.COM

Special thanks to my technical advisers for their professional contribution.

Steve Nawojczyk (Na-VOY-check) - Retired in 1994 as Pulaski County Coroner in Little Rock, Arkansas and has served as advisor to the Arkansas Attorney General's Youth Gang Task Force since 1993. With a background as coroner in two Arkansas counties and former Director of the Arkansas State Crime Laboratory, Steve has over twenty years experience in death investigation. Steve has been researching gangs and other juvenile violence since 1987. His work has been featured in the New York Times, Jobs - A Way Out? PBS's Act Against Violence campaign, and on HBO in the America Undercover series, Gang War: Bangin' in Little Rock, the 1994 Cable Ace award winner for best documentary. He has made appearances on the Phil Donahue Show, CBS News Up to the Minute, CBS This Morning, Larry King Live, BBC-TV network, the syndicated shows Tough Target and Save Our Streets and National Public Radio. Steve has acted as consultant to then-Governor Bill Clinton, the offices of the United States Attorney, the U.S. Army War College, Ohio State University's Fellows in Criminal Justice Program, The National Association of Attorneys General, The National Society for Human Resource Management, the National Education Association School Safety Summit, and numerous other collegiate institutions, school officials and other communities on the dynamics of gangs and youth violence. Steve has been consistently evaluated as the highest rated speaker in hundreds of conferences throughout the United States.

His presentations have been described as motivational and inspirational, touching both the heart and cognitive mind, thorough and exceptionally thought provoking, answering so many questions and opening a world of concern, and enlightening, outstanding and beyond excellence.

Jared Lewis
Director of Know Gangs

Since 1997, Know Gangs has been a leading training provider for law enforcement, educators and social service workers seeking to enhance their knowledge about gangs, drugs and school violence.

While serving as a police officer in California, Jared Lewis created the organization in an effort to better assist his coworkers with additional information and resources about gangs and dealing with gang-affiliated individuals. Since that time Know Gangs and it's instructors has trained thousands of professionals throughout the world. In 2003, Know Gangs moved from Modesto, California to its current location in Jefferson, Wisconsin. For more information visit Jared Lewis's website at www.knowgangs.com

Dan R. Miller, Ph.D. - More than thirty years of solid hands-on experience along with advanced degrees, have given Dr. Miller the insight needed to deal with the security problems and opportunities facing us today. Dr. Miller has been a street police officer. He has been a police union officer, and in the private sector, the company officer responsible for union avoidance. He was a correctional officer in a large state prison, where he worked in every position from gun tower to the "hole". In the contract security field, he was responsible for security guard operations and investigations. He was Director of Corporate Personnel and Security for a large retail chain, and later for a multi-state financial institution. He served on management, human resource and strategic planning committees in these and other roles, and has published in several fields. He is a U. S. Army veteran. Couple this with a few years as a butcher and meat department manager in New York City, several years as an undercover police officer for which he won many awards and commendations including one presented by the Governor of North Carolina, one presented by a former District Attorney, who later became Chief Justice of the North Carolina Supreme Court, Assistant District Attorneys, and others from Mayors, Councils, and Police Chiefs, and you have a real blend of education, experience, and street and people savvy. Dan is on the regular Criminal Justice faculty at Bethune-Cookman University. Previously he taught at The University of North Carolina at Charlotte and Barber-Scotia College. He has a natural flair for communicating in a lively, interesting, and entertaining way. Dr. Miller is the president and founder of CompleteSecurity1.com in Daytona Beach, Florida.

Ari K. Bolden - Founder of Veritas Night Club Services in 2001, after recognizing the need for proper nightclub security training. That following year, in 2002, he published "The Doorman's Credo: A Guide for Nightclub Security" to better aid those in the profession. Two years later, with the help and guidance of Darren Laur (owner of Personal Protection Systems), he officially launched his nightclub security seminars. Ari holds his degree in Philosophy (ethics) from the University of Victoria, graduated top in his class in 2001 from the Private Investigators Association of British Columbia (PIABC) through Douglas College, has a media and public relations background of five years (radio broadcasting), is first aid certified, and a martial arts practitioner (20 years) and holds black belt rankings in arts of Jiu Jitsu and Aikido. He currently teaches Jiu Jitsu through his other company, the Bujitsu Academy of Victoria. Ari has worked in several venues over the past 10 years and currently is the head of security for the largest liquor venue in B.C. His intuitive nature and high level of professionalism has allowed him to gain a vast amount of knowledge of the industry. His particular areas of expertise are people management, conflict resolution, physical restraints, and the legalities of the hospitality industry.

Melvin A Cardonell-

Rockin' Mel Cardonell has over 20 years of experience in the field of Nightclub & Bar security and over half of these years have been spent working in Biker Bars. At over 6 ft tall and 300 lbs, a truly gentle giant Mel has an excellent working knowledge of biker bar security. He is known and respected by both the Independent and outlaw bikers that frequent his bar. Mel attended Kaplan University and received certification in Anti-Terrorism and National Security Management. Mel is currently studying for his Associates Degree in Criminal Justice at Kaplan University. A registered bodyguard with SEAL Bodyguard International. Mel has provided executive protection for Nascar drivers, Authors, Movie Stars, Rock Bands, Professional Athletes and Professional Wrestlers and Private Business Owners. Mel holds a State of Florida Class C Security License and State of Florida Class CC Private Investigator License. He is currently pursuing his State of Florida Class G Armed Security License. A member in good standing with the Florida Association of Private Investigators. Mel is a certified Instructor with the National Nightclub Protection Council.
Mel has studied Northern Chinese Shaolin Kung Fu. In addition has an Instructor's Certification in American Goju Ryu Karate
Mel has been Chief of Security at two of the world's largest Biker Bar Organizations.

Special thanks to my loving wife Shirley for her love, support and assistance during the writing of this book.

Foreword

It was a newspaper outside my door that first alerted me to this unspeakable crime. The words: 'Club Bouncer Is Arraigned in Murder of Graduate Student'. At a club in New York called the 'Falls Bar' a bouncer Darryl Littlejohn, 41, strangled a graduate student while trying to rape and sexually assault her, then dumped her body in a vacant lot near the Belt Parkway. The arraignment of the bouncer, on first-degree murder charges came about a month after the body of Imette St. Guillen, 24, a student at John Jay College of criminal justice was found. Later it was revealed that Daniel Dorrian, the son of the bar's co-owner Jack Dorrian, knew that the bouncer he hired was a paroled violent felon. It was also stated that Littlejohn was a suspect in several other abductions and rapes. Though my own investigation I came to understand that the Dorrian family are well known bar owners who have several nightclubs and bars in the NY area. Any logical person with an ounce of common sense can read Immette's story and see that Darryl Littlejohn was a sociopath working as a bouncer, for a bar owner who acknowledged but disregarded his violent traits. Thus a criminal background check would of revealed Littlejohn's criminal past but it is useless if the bar owners ignore the details. Why a bar owner would hire an aggressive ex-con to take care of his patrons and staff members is beyond reason. The Fall's Bar has been shutdown since the incident. On February 1, 2007, I read that Immette's family filed a lawsuit targeting not only Littlejohn but also the bar owners who employed him.

I have advocated for many years that Bar and nightclub owner's need to be held accountable if we hope to bring to an end the hiring of security personnel who have violent dispositions. Bouncers/Doormen have always had a reputation that is shaded in controversy. But then, so do other professions such as law enforcement, and the military.

However it is the responsibility of the true professional's in any trade to make an effort to ensure the highest standards and ethics are enforced and utilized. For this particular reason, I wrote this training guide with the support of fellow professionals in their respected fields of expertise. Thus, this manual is based on a thesis type methodology. History has taught us that to survive extinction, one must evolve. The Art of Bouncing is no different. If we do not progress, relinquish erroneous logic and become the elite in our trade, we will be replaced with a perfunctory security system. My overall aspiration is that young men and women looking to pursue a career in nightclub security will do so with a proper mindset and respect for those of us who have given so much to the trade.

CONTENTS

Introduction:

The Origin of Bouncing

Civilization begins with order, grows with liberty, and dies with chaos.

Will Durant (1885 - 1981)

When bouncing came to be no one really knows for sure. However, it is my hypothesis that when man's existence began no independent security system existed because of early man's 'Tribal Mentality'. In the distant past, human beings lived a primitive lifestyle. Dwelling in caves and jungles, they hunted to survive. Since resources were limited, they were vulnerable to malnutrition and starvation, sudden death from natural disasters or attacks by wild animals. For their survival and growth they lived in small tribes whose members protected each other. While the men hunted with their arrows and spears, their women looked after the children and animals. Such a lifestyle created a tribal mentality. Each tribe saw other tribes as potential enemies who would attack them and steal their women, children and animals. To protect their limited resources they were always ready for tribal wars. Killing members of another tribe could start a tribal war that continued for generations in which innocent men, women and children were killed for revenge. Sometimes the goal was not only to kill but also to humiliate. Rather than dispatching their adversaries quickly, they would torture their enemy captives so that they died a painful humiliating death and /or displayed the dead body in such a manner that would send a thought-provoking message to their enemies. In the last few thousand years human beings have made progress in many aspects of life but in other areas they are still very primitive in their beliefs and attitudes. In the 21st century human beings may live in skyscrapers in huge cities, travel in cars, trains and planes, and communicate around the planet by telephone and Internet, as members of a worldwide global village.

But many human beings have neither evolved in their minds nor grown in their personalities. They still have a tribal mentality—all that has changed is the definition of the tribe and the nature of tribal war.

A modern example of the tribal mentality would be Organized Crime in the form of street gangs, motorcycle gangs, prison gangs, Mafias, Cartels...etc.

A cycle of violence and tribal war can take place between two ordinary people, their families, two heads of state, two gang leaders who perceive each other as enemies or a potential threat. As the war continues both enemies pass on their tribal mindset to the next generation who, once brainwashed join the tribal war started by their elders and previous generations. It is distressing to see that when the cycle of violence continues and tribal war is maintained, people on both sides start identifying with the opponent to acquire the psychological profile of the enemy. They begin to emulate each other's behavior and political viewpoint in order to 'fight the good fight'.

Roman Empire (27 BC - 1453): Bouncing only could have evolved when mankind established communal and privileged gathering places that hosted associations as well as individual members. We find record of this type of formal gathering in the time of the Roman Empire Associations that evidenced strong bonds among its members. It was common to find kinship language used within the group, with members referred to as "brothers" and leaders designated as "fathers" or "mothers." These strong bonds were also expressed by the use of such a designation as "friends" for the associates of the group.

The communal bond itself was often designated by the term koinon and its cognates. It would be misleading, however, to suggest that internal community relations were completely amicable. We have, in fact, abundant evidence to the contrary. Inscriptions were often set up outlining the internal community regulations of associations. Members were warned against such abuses as "disorderliness" (akosmeÆ), taking another member's seat, insulting another member (or a member's mother), or physically abusing another. In general, failure to meet the moral or communal standards set by the association would result in one or more of any number of the following punishments: fines, flogging, restrictions from the association's rituals, temporary expulsion, or loss of membership. In some cases, a special group of 'Bouncers' were used to keep order and remove violators of the association's regulations.

RENAISSANCE (1400-1600): An intellectual revolution that promoted the careful reading of the authors of ancient Greece and Rome, applying their concepts to a changing society. Ironically, despite this growth in intellectual practice, this period also saw writers justify the witch-hunts, which were just beginning to intensify. The magical tendencies of Neoplatonic philosophy, alchemy and astrology, such as by Giovanni Pico Della Mirandola, might have promoted an atmosphere of credulity in the supernatural. During this period of time pubs and brothels flourished. If bouncers were employed during this period of time Swordsmanship would have been a priority in the area of self-defense. The idea that Medieval and Renaissance swordsmen were primitive is far from true. Rather, their combat methods were very sophisticated. The insights shown in many Renaissance writings on sword techniques and dynamics point to this, especially since the surest route to fortune traditionally rested on developing better methods for Europeans to kill each other. Many have the image of the crude, barbarian, sword- wielding knights and don't stop to consider that some of the knights would also be the rich elite who went to college and studied Greek, Latin, and Mathematics. They'd also had a keen interest in understanding the science of local motions, pendulum motions and impacts which might be at least part of the reason that the aristocracy was sponsoring a great deal of research in the field of swordsmanship. At the time, there arose in Europe a distinction between those swords intended for war and those for personal self-defense. Social forces had begun to allow commoners to not only be able to afford and legally own their own swords, but to wear them in the crowded and expanding cities. Additionally, the transformation of warfare by firearms and the breakdown of the old feudal order limited the avenues for both redress of personal grievance and exhibition of martial skill. The result was an explosion in the popularity of dueling. This in turn caused a renewed interest in the personal "Art of the Sword". Combined with the new "sciences" then coming into vogue, a systematic approach to studying swordsmanship swept Western Europe. This was to climax later in the methods of the "cut & thrust sword" and the development of its cousin, the thrusting "rapier" with its unique manner of fence. Based on earlier medieval traditions, new schools of swordsmanship sprang up all across Europe in the Renaissance. Many schools of fencing had unsavory reputations as hangouts for "ruffians and hoodlums". Still, many well respected and highly sought-after instructors or "Masters of Defense" as they were known, became well respected. In Germany there were numerous "fectmiesters" (fight masters) and long-lived fighting guilds such as the "Marxbrueder" and the "Federfechter". They specialized primarily in long-swords and two-handed swords and later, rapiers. Henry the VII made official a consolidated school of fencing (primarily for sword & buckler) as a legal guild in 1540. Following the tradition of the old English masters-at-arms, it was known as the "Corporation of the Masters of the Noble Science of Defense" (or just the "London Company of Masters"). It specialized in a range of weaponry and had four levels of student: scholar, free scholar, provost and master. Italian and Spanish rapier instructors were eventually also among the most admired across Europe. It is a myth that Renaissance sword fighting used a brutal, artless approach.

Examination of the historical texts and artwork of the period clearly dismisses this prejudice.

Few individuals outside of historical-fencers and Medievalists are aware that literally dozens of rare and obscure manuscripts on swordsmanship and fighting arts by European masters still survive. During their age, Masters of Defense such as Agrippa, Morrozo, Capo Ferro, George Silver, Joseph Swetnam, Fabris, Saviolo, di Grassi, Sutor, Alfieri, and many others were highly regarded experts. They published their methods and teachings in numerous illustrated technical manuals. These invaluable works present a highly developed and innovative aspect of Renaissance martial culture. They reveal swordsmanship at the time to be a systematic and highly dynamic art, far from being uniform. Among the most famous and influential of the works on the earlier cut & thrust method are those of the Italian Masters such as Castiglione in 1528, Mancolino's in 1531, Achille Marozzo in 1536 and Altoni in 1550. Some of the earlier Medieval German fechtbuchs ("fight books"), such as Talhoffer's of 1443 and Lebkommer's of 1530, also contain elements of cut & thrust techniques in their instructions. Among the most noted practitioners of the cut & thrust method was the Englishman George Silver, who wrote books in 1598 and 1599 ("Paradoxes of Defense" and "Brief Instructions..."). Silver and his brother like many Masters of Defense of the time also taught wrestling, use of the two-handed sword, dagger-fighting, staffs and pole-arms. Techniques for grappling and disarming had been a common part of the curriculum in any school of arms since the Middle Ages.

1800 -1900: In US Western towns in the 1870s, high-class brothels known as "good houses" or "parlor houses" hired bouncers for security and to prevent patrons from evading payment.

"Good house"-style brothel's…considered themselves the cream of the crop, and [the prostitutes working there] scorned those who worked in (or out of) saloons, dance halls, and theaters. The best bordellos looked like respectable mansions with attractively decorated parlors, a game room and a dance hall. For security, somewhere in every parlor house there was always a bouncer; a giant of a man who stayed sober to handle any customer who got too rough with one of the girls or didn't want to pay his bill. The " protective presence" of bouncers in high-class brothels was "…one of the reasons the girls considered themselves superior to [lower-class] free-lancers, who lacked any such shepherds. Thus in the times of the Wild West, bouncers were armed and hired for their reputations in Saloons, Whorehouses and Gambling halls. Many under the same roof. For example, over 20 years after the Civil War, cowboys coaxed herds of cattle along arduous trails from the Texas grasslands north to the railheads in Kansas. At the end of the trail lay the infamous cow towns, places such as Abilene, Hays City, Wichita, Ellsworth and Dodge City. After following a slow moving herd of cattle along a dusty trail for as many as three months, these towns offered the cowboy a place to take a bath, gamble, find a woman, eat some good food and let off some steam. The towns accommodated their visitors with a liberal attitude towards their boisterous behavior. There were limits, however, and the towns hired enforcers to maintain a semblance of law and order. Law officers such as Wyatt Earp, Wild Bill Hickok, Luke Short and Bat Masterson became legends.

The "Dodge City Peace Commission" June 1883.

From left to right, standing: W.H. Harris, Luke Short,

Bat Masterson, W.F. Petillon.

Seated: Charlie Bassett, Wyatt Earp, Frank McLain and Neal Brown.

Alexander Franklin "Frank" James was born January 10, 1843 in Kearney, Missouri. Some say that he was the real leader of the James Gang. In the summer of 1862 Frank joined "Bloody" Bill Anderson's gang at age 19. On parole as a member of the Confederate Rome Guard unit that fought at Wilson's Creek, he deserted or left because of illness. In June of 1874 he married Anna Ralston. The trial of Frank James took place at Huntsville, Alabama. Before 1900, Frank James was working at the Standard Theatre in St. Louis as an usher, doorman, and bouncer. On March 30, 1900 Frank James gave a testimonial performance at the Standard Theatre. Frank ran a museum out of the James place in his old age. On February 15 (some sources state February 18), 1915 Frank James died of a heart attack at the age of 72 in Kearney. His family tried to hide or disguise his grave because he feared that his body would be dug up and experiments run on his brain. He had heard that this had happened to his brother Jesse. Frank is buried in Hill Park Cemetery, Independence, Missouri.

In the Wisconsin lumberjack days, bouncers would physically remove drinkers who were too drunk to keep buying drinks and thus free up space in the bar for new patrons. The slang term 'snake-room' was used to describe a "...room off a saloon, usually two or three steps down, into which a bar-keeper or the bouncer could slide drunk lumberjacks head first through swinging doors from the bar room." In the late 1800s, until Prohibition, bouncers also had the unusual role of protecting the saloon's buffet. To attract business, "...many saloons lured customers with offers of a "free lunch"—usually well salted to inspire drinking, and the saloon bouncer was generally on hand to discourage, those with too hearty an appetite". In the late 1800s, bouncers at small town dances and bars physically resolved disputes and removed troublemakers without worrying about lawsuits. In the main bar in one Iowa town, "...there were many quarrels, many fights, but all were settled on the spot. There were no court costs for the bouncers or the bar, only some aches and pains for the troublemakers". It is said that the word "bouncer" was first used in the saloon sense in an 1883 newspaper article wrote:

"'The Bouncer' is merely the English 'chucker out'. When liberty verges on license and gaiety on wanton delirium, the Bouncer selects the gayest of the gay, and - bounces him!" (Note: that 'gay' is used in the older sense of 'happy', or in this case, 'too rowdy')

In the 1930s, the bawdiest parts of Baltimore, Maryland near the docks were filled with "burlesque shows, penny arcades, tattoo parlors, saloons, cheap hotels fifth-rate movies, night clubs and shooting galleries." Bars in this rough neighborhood filled with sailors and dockworkers hired bouncers as physical enforcers to maintain order and eject aggressive patrons. The Oasis club, operated by Max Cohen hired a lady bouncer by the name of Mickey Steele, a six-foot acrobat from the Pennsylvania coal fields. Mickey was always considerate of the people she bounced; first asking them where they lived and then throwing them in that general direction. She was succeeded by a character known as 'Machine-Gun Butch'" who was a long-time bouncer at the club".

Other famous bouncers of yesterday and today

Christopher Michael Langan - worked various times as a cowboy, firefighter, construction worker and for the past 20+ years, as a bar bouncer in assorted nightclubs across the East End of Long Island. Without benefit of formal higher education, he has engaged for over two decades in research on mathematics, physics, cosmology and the cognitive sciences. He has a tested IQ of over 200.

Mr. T - (born Laurence Tureaud, May 21, 1952) is an actor mostly known for his roles in the 1980s television series The A-Team and as boxer Clubber Lang in the 1982 film Rocky III. In 1982 Sylvester Stallone spotted Mr. T while taking part in "The World's Toughest Bouncer" contest.

Dolph Lundgren- former karate champion turned action film star, most famously the superbly trained, steroid-enhanced Russian boxer Drago in "Rocky IV" (1985), his feature "debut".

"Scarface "Al Capone - one of the most famous U.S. gangsters during the 1930s, a Chicago-based boss involved in illegal gambling, bootlegging (illegal alcohol) and prostitution. Capone got his start in New York, working as a thug and bouncer (where he got the three scars that spawned his nickname, "Scarface").

Chazz Palminteri - New York-born and raised movie actor. He was a natural choice to bring grit, muscle and an evocative realism to the sidewalks of his New York neighborhood, violent as they were. Born in 1952, Palminteri grew up in a tough area of the Bronx and it gave young Calogero (Palminteri's given first name) the life lessons that would later prove very useful. He graduated from Theodore Roosevelt High School and worked as a bouncer and doorman in nightclubs, among other jobs before breaking into movies.

Sylvester Stallone – The star of 'ROCKY' . When he was 15, Stallone and his mother moved to Philadelphia, the setting of Rocky. Soon bored with the street-gamy life there, he took off for Europe and landed a job as a bouncer in the girls' dorm of The American School of Switzerland. The highlight of his bouncing career came when he chaperoned a group of girls on a visit to Paris, boarded them in a cheap inn and pocketed most of the ample hotel money. "What the hell," he says. "They saw the real Paris that way."

Mark Vincent – was raised by his astrologer/psychologist mother and adoptive father in an artist's housing project in New York's Greenwich Village, never knowing his biological father. At 17 and already sporting a well-honed physique, he became a bouncer at some of New York's hippest clubs to earn himself some extra cash. He worked a total of 9 years as a bouncer. It was at this time that he changed his name to 'Vin Diesel'.

A young Jack Dempsey was once the bartender and the bouncer at the still popular Mizpah Hotel and Casino in Nevada.

Ezzard Charles - Over the course of his professional boxing career, had 122 bouts with 96 wins, 25 losses and one draw. Charles tried several jobs after the end of his boxing days. He was a safety inspector for the State of Ohio and then a bouncer at a Northern Kentucky nightclub.

Chapter One:

The Nightclub Security Professional

'Being a professional is doing the things you love to do, on

the days you don't feel like doing them.'

-Julius Erving

"What do you see when you look into the face of a nightclub doorman? The Bouncer. A fighter? A bully? A hard man of repute? I bet you don't see a husband; father; a brother; a son. People think that working the door is easy. They sit there with plank in their eye looking at you like you are a piece of shit. A baby eater or a f*cking serial killer. They don't think that when you are pulling some f*cking lump off them whose gonna kill them."

-From Geoff Thompson's "The Bouncer"

I know Geoff Thompson as a bouncer loyal to the trade and a professional who never pulls any punches. Geoff is an excellent example of a bouncer from the old school, who continues to gain wisdom though experience. Nightclub security has many facets. Every person works the door for different reasons and in various ways. But there are really no set guidelines on how one should run security in a nightclub or bar. Yes we have rules and regulations mandated by ABT or ABC. But beyond the local liquor laws the rest of the trade is a gray area. What is the job of the bouncer/doorman? I refer to the job as the 4 P's that denote the meaning 'Protection of Personnel, Patrons and Property'. But the word protection has its different meaning for each individual person.

pro·tec·tion n.

1.a. The act of protecting.

  b. The condition of being protected.

2. One that protects.

3. A pass guaranteeing safe-conduct to travelers.

4. A system of tariffs or other measures protecting domestic producers from foreign competition.

5. A contraceptive or barrier that lowers the risk of pregnancy or infection, especially a condom.

6. Slang

  a. Money extorted by racketeers threatening violence for nonpayment.

  b. Bribes paid to officials by racketeers for immunity from prosecution.

As one can see protection can be either right or wrong. Given the perspective in number 1, 2 & 3 or following the viewpoint contained in number 6. A person's bouncing ability is in direct correlation to his personality, mindset and temperament. What makes a good bouncer is having an equal balance of mental and physical ability. What makes a great bouncer is having complete control over both abilities. A Bouncer/Doorman should take pride in what he does. He should conduct himself in a professional manner while on duty at all times. Being a professional is taking your job seriously. **Bouncing is not 'A' job- it is 'THE' job**. You have to look at the trade in the appropriate perspective.

Metaphorically speaking – you are a bodyguard protecting a crowd of people for your employer. By the way, many bouncers get hired as bodyguards because they have a solid foundation when it comes to protection. We are not only protecting the patrons from other's but from their own self-defeating actions as well. Thus the Doorman/Bouncer must approach his job with genuineness and a want to perform his duties to the best of his ability. A zero tolerance is given to doormen/bouncers that think they are getting paid to stand around, chat with their buddies or chase women all night. Worse yet, are security personnel who like to fight, start fights and/or drink liquor while on the job. The most inexcusable conduct is when nightclub security gangs up and seriously injures an intoxicated patron and/or sell narcotics in the nightclub. As Ari Bolden states in his book 'The Doorman Credo'- "what I always tell managers or head doorman is: "The failings of your door staff is a direct correlation to how you run your team. As a doorman, you have to set the level of professionalism at your establishment. " The Doorman is the first person the patron sees when he enters the club and thus indirectly sets the tempo for the style and attitude of the club. Some clubs employ huge muscle bound individuals. Other clubs use well-dressed ladies and gentlemen to make patrons feel like they have entered a fashionable nightclub. The true function of a doorman is to provide access control for the nightclub and screen those that enter.

A doorman is traditionally the person who stands at the door and checks IDs to assure that each patron is of age to legally enter the establishment and is dressed appropriately should the club have a dress code. In some nightclubs, doormen use metal detectors, do bag inspections and perform pat downs where the format attracts mostly young patrons or is prone to gang activity. Another function of a doorman is to prevent admittance to those that are obviously intoxicated or who have previously caused trouble inside the club. Most clubs have an "86" policy where disorderly patrons are barred from returning to the club for a designated period of time. In some severe cases police are called and a 'Trespass Warrant' is issued. Depending on the club, a doorman can be used to collect cover charges, tickets, or direct patrons to tables. In addition to normal doorman duties, some nightclubs use the door staff to monitor patron conduct on the sidewalk as well as inside the club. The nature of this additional task can lead to confrontations with aggressive nightclub patrons if not handled professionally. Most busy nightclubs begin to have problems when the club has too few security personnel or when employing inexperienced and poorly trained doorman.

Bouncer Vs Doorman: Is there a difference?

The main reason for the difference in the name or title is basically "Political Correctness". In the past, a bouncer was viewed as a huge, muscle bound guy who threw people out of nightclubs for breaking the rules. The bouncer had very little social skills and relied upon brawn rather than brains to operate. Bouncers are an enigma so to speak. The term bouncer presents an image of a brawler who will break up fights and forcibly eject obnoxious patrons.

Bouncers are often portrayed in movies as tough guys and rebels who love to fight, like in the movie "Roadhouse". Many nightclubs foster that image by hiring large - bodybuilders, football players, wrestlers or martial artists to handle drunk or out of control patrons. Usually this type of bouncer has little or no experience and has receive no real formal training in area's of nightclub security or State liquor laws. In a crisis these inexperienced bouncers will be forced to rely on their own common sense and instincts to solve a problem. This metaphorically speaking is like adding fuel to a fire. A doorman on the other hand, is considered a Public Relations /people person type bouncer. They are hired to make sure that the patrons have an enjoyable and safe night. Always the gentleman, the Doorman still enforces the rules, but they are seen as the more modern "thinking-man's bouncer." Owners wanted the public to see their security as customer service professionals (which they are) so the title 'Doorman' was introduced some time in the 1990's. The owners also believe that in a court of law should an incident occur involving there security personnel, "Doorman" sounded better and less aggressive than "Bouncer". But upon personal research it is revealed that it is irrelevant if a person is called a bouncer, doorman or cooler. For it is the actions of the person that will hold him or her accountable. Regardless of the title, the duty of a bouncer/doorman remains the same, to monitor the crowd to see that everyone follows the rules and regulations of the establishment. The goal should be to see that everyone has a good time, but within established limits. A bouncer protects his patrons, staff and his employer's property. Professional bouncers/doormen are personable, friendly and can converse with people without appearing threatening or intimidating. The professional bouncer doesn't "bounce" anyone…they communicate with their patrons and fellow staff members. The mere presence of a well-trained security team will remind the patrons that their conduct is being observed and that they need to obey the rules and regulations of the club.

What is the function of a Doorman?

- To represent your nightclub in a professional manner at all times.
- To implement the rules and regulations mandated by ABT, ABC and local Law Enforcement that pertain to your function in the nightclub.
- To protect fellow staff members from harm and abuse.
- To protect patrons from harm and abuse.
- To protect the property of your employer from damage.

The Reality of the Profession

Being a Doorman/Bouncer can fluctuate from quiet- to easy going- to vigorous -to dangerous. There is no set pattern or degree. A quiet night can become active-aggressive by the arrival of a few rough patrons. It can also go from vigorous to very dangerous by the arrival of aggressive street gang members or violent felons. You are employed in a line of work where bad attitudes, active-aggressive personalities, excessive consumption of alcohol and drug abuse are accepted as the social norm. It is your job to enforce the 4 P's and the rules and regulations mandated by ABT, ABC and local Law Enforcement that pertain to your function in the nightclub.

A Doorman/Bouncer must be able to defend him/herself and protect others. He/she must be able to say alert late into the night and work long hours standing or walking. Eyesight must be good to ensure that one can observe activities in a semi-dark club at various distances. Just so you understand, here are a few things that have happened to myself and my fellow professionals while working as a doorman/bouncer. We have been punched, kicked, grabbed, bitten, spat on and hit with bottles, chairs, pool cues and tables. We have had weapons of all types pulled on us, everything from chains, baseball bats, stun guns, pepper spray, knives and firearms. I myself have been shot and cut twice and poisoned once. If you are seriously thinking about becoming a bouncer/doorman, you should know that this profession can bring a heavy toll to one's life. It certainly isn't all just good times, women and music. You'll have to guard yourself from getting jaded and bitter. You will see abuse, violence, drugs, lewd sex acts, alcoholism, and sometimes even death. The nightclub scene is very political in nature; treachery and deceit are always present. It is very much a 'high school mentality' where gossip and countless rumors can easily damage one's personal life and reputation. Make sure you possess a strong mindset and stick to your professional standards at all times when you decide to become a doorman/bouncer or you will fall prey to the temptations and negativity that can impair a professional's judgment. A bouncer/doorman must be in control of him/herself at all times. If you have a bad temper, don't like to socialize, like to fight, looking to be in a position of authority to boost your ego. Do yourself and others a favor and <u>do not become a bouncer/doorman.</u> We have far too many egotistical adrenaline junkies in nightclubs today posing as nightclub security. It is only a matter of time before Government and State regulations weed out these imposters who continue to afflict the dignity of our profession.

Chapter Two:

The Establishment

It is my philosophical belief that a nightclub or bar is the communal watering hole of humanity. It is this social gathering that quenches not only the physical but also the psychological thirst of the social animal.

Ivan 'Doc' Holiday

There are many different types of establishments that serve alcohol and entertainment to the public and use security.

- Nightclubs
- Pubs
- Bars
- Taverns
- Saloons
- Lounges
- Roadhouses
- Strip Clubs
- Gentlemen's Clubs
- Dance halls
- Discos
- Country bars
- Hip Hop Clubs
- Gothic Clubs
- Rock clubs
- Blues Clubs
- Jazz Clubs
- Biker Bars
- Bottle clubs
- Techno Clubs
- After Hours Clubs
- Rave clubs

- Private Clubs
- Casino Bars
- Music Concerts
- Sport bars
- Comedy Clubs
- Gay Clubs
- Super Clubs (Clubs owned by a Major Record Label)

Regardless of the club, employing trained security personnel is a must and 90% of these establishments employ some type security. Establishments vary not only in their music, theme or design but in how they are organize and managed. The classification of a bar or nightclub will dictate the type of patrons that will come there. For example a cowboy club will have a Saloon type theme and will play a majority of country music.

The music itself can vary as well as the customers; case in point, a hardcore biker may like country music. But for the greater part, bars with a set theme mostly attract their own customary clientele. Thus before you decide to take a security job with a nightclub or bar there are some things you need to consider. What is the reputation of the club? Does the club have a bad reputation for fights, over excessive security personnel, gangs, drugs, excessive violence…etc. Has anyone employed at this club ever been seriously hurt on the job. What is the atmosphere of the club? Is it busy, slow, fair? What type of crowd? Old, young, middle-aged. Who owns the club and who operates the club? Is the manager the owner or does he have someone else manage it.

Does the person who manages the club have a good working relationship with his patrons and employees? What is the security like? Is the Cooler/Head of security a professional? Are the security personnel experienced? Do they work as a team or individuals? Will they provide trustworthy backup? What is the nightclub or bar's operating procedure? For example, the hours of operations, hours and days worked per week, duties of each staff member. What are your duties? How many hours do you work and what is the pay scale. Do they have any kind of medical and dental coverage should you become injured on the job?

When looking for a nightclub security position at a club, drop by the club on a Friday night, go in as a patron and watch. Feel the place out. This is the number one way to know what is going on in the club. On the second night (Saturday) talk to the security, bartender and other staff members (If they are not to busy). Last, if you feel that the club is a place where you would like to work talk to the Head of Security or ask to see the manager. **But always talk to the cooler first.** It shows respect for his position, regardless if he is the hiring authority or not. When looking for a job, dress well and have a good resume that pertains to the position you are applying for. The most important part of your resume is good solid references that can be easily reached. Also a phone number and/or email address where you can be contacted. In this era of advanced telecommunications, there is absolutely no reason to make contacting you difficult for the potential employer. Give the potential employer your cell phone number, even if you have to buy a mobile for your job search. Avoid the futile phone tag that may make you miss out on an interview or the job altogether.

Write and customize a "goal" for each job and employer. The goal is your opportunity to connect your particular skills, experience, traits, and job requirements with those the employer is seeking. Thus by first checking out the nightclub or bar you can pick out exactly what the employer believes he needs. For example if you're checking out a country bar, you design your resume to emphasize your particular proficiency and knowledge of security in country clubs. The purpose of a resume is to get you the all-important interview. When granted an interview remember the 4-P's. NEVER discuss fighting or such related subject matter. NEVER bad-mouth other clubs or club owners. Be polite, professional and present yourself as a team player. When hired make sure you understand fully how the cooler and the manager want the security to function. Overall the most important thing to remember is do not hire on to a club or bar that exceeds your abilities or knowledge.

How to build a well-organized resume

Resume Essentials

Before you write, take time to do a self-assessment on paper.
Outline your skills and abilities as well as your work experience and
extracurricular activities. This will make it easier to prepare a thorough
resume.

The Content of Your Resume

Name, address, telephone, e-mail address, web site address
All your contact information should go at the top of your resume.
Avoid nicknames.
Use a permanent address. Use your parents' address, a friend's
address, or the address you plan to use after graduation.
Use a permanent telephone number and include the area code. If you
have an answering machine, record a neutral greeting.
Add your e-mail address. Many employers will find it useful. (Note:
Choose an e-mail address that sounds professional.)
Include your web site address only if the web page reflects your
professional ambitions.

Education

New graduates without a lot of work experience should list their educational information first. Alumni can list it after the work experience section.

Your most recent educational information is listed first.

Include your degree (A.S., B.S., B.A., etc.), major, institution attended, minor/concentration.

Add your grade point average (GPA) if it is higher than 3.0.

Mention academic honors.

Work Experience

Briefly give the employer an overview of work that has taught you skills. Use 'action' words to describe your job duties. Include your work experience in reverse chronological order—that is, put your last job first and work backward to your first, relevant job. Include:

Title of position,

Name of organization

Location of work (town, state)

Dates of employment

Describe your work responsibilities with emphasis on specific skills and achievements.

Other information

You may want to add:

Special training, skills or competencies,

Leadership experience in volunteer organizations,

Participation in sports.

References

Ask people if they are willing to serve as references before you give their names to a potential employer.

Always try to use references that pertain to your trade and are highly regarded.

Include your reference information on your resume at the end.

Content:

Run a spell check on your computer before anyone sees your resume.

Get a friend to proofread. The more people who see your resume, the more likely that misspelled words and awkward phrases will be seen (and corrected).

Design:

These tips will make your resume easier to read and/or scan into an employer's database.

Use white or off-white paper.

Use 8-1/2- x 11-inch paper.

Print on one side of the paper.

Use a font size of 12 to 14 points.

Use non-decorative typefaces.

Choose one typeface and stick to it.

Avoid italics, script, and underlined words.

Do not use horizontal or vertical lines, graphics, or shading.

Do not fold or staple your resume.

If you must mail your resume, put it in a large envelope.

Chapter Three

Bouncer Gear

Humble words and increased preparations are signs
that the enemy is about to advance. Violent language
and driving forward as if to the attack are signs that he
will retreat.

SunTzu – Art of War

The most important factor in a nightclub or bar is **Safety**.

To apply the **4-P's – Protection of Patrons, Personnel, and Property** one must have not only the ability but also the tools needed to perform the task. Every establishment must and should have commercial grade Fire Extinguishers and a proper First-Aid Kit. As a professional before you start your shift you need to always inspect the Fire Extinguisher's to make sure they are fully charged and the inspection tags are up to date. Also ensure that all Fire Exits are open and unblocked.

The following story is an example of inadequate safety and incompetent security.

The Station Nightclub Fire

The fire started about 11:08 PM, just seconds into headlining band Great White's opening song "Desert Moon", when pyrotechnics set off by their tour manager, Daniel Biechele, lit flammable soundproofing foam behind the stage. The flames were first thought to be part of the act; only as the fire reached the ceiling and smoke began to billow did people realize it was uncontrolled. Only 20 seconds after the pyrotechnics ended, the band stopped playing, and lead singer, Jack Russell, remarked into the microphone, "Wow... this ain't good." In less than a minute, the entire stage was engulfed in flames. Although there were four possible exits, most people naturally headed for the door through which they entered. The ensuing stampede in the inferno led to a crush in the hallway leading to that main entrance, eventually blocking it completely and resulting in numerous deaths and injuries among the patrons and staff, who numbered somewhat more than 404, the highest of three conflicting official capacity limits.

 Of those in attendance, roughly one quarter died (either from burns or smoke inhalation), and half were injured. Among those who perished in the fire was Great White's lead guitarist, Ty Longley. The pyrotechnics were gerbs, cylindrical devices intended to produce a controlled spray of sparks. Gerbs are labeled using two numbers: one for how far the sparks fly and one for how long the effect lasts. Biechele was fond of using 15 by 15's, which spray sparks 15 feet for 15 seconds. Three of that same caliber, at 45-degree angles, with the middle one pointing straight up, were the kind used that night. Gerbs are considered appropriate for indoor use before a nearby audience when proper precautions are observed. But Great White did not have the required city permit for a pyrotechnics display, officials said later. An NIST investigation of the fire, using computer simulations and a mock-up of the stage area and dance floor, concluded that a sprinkler system would have successfully contained the fire enough to give everyone time to get out safely. However, due to its age (built in the late 1930s) and size (4,484 square feet (404 m²)), the Station was not required to have a sprinkler system, and it was not equipped with one. Also the blueprints show that the entryway to the nightclub had a ramp, which blocked off a straight exit way through the door. When exiting the building, one would have to exit either right or left because the building was constructed to lead two entryways with the handrail running parallel with the building. Investigators focused on the foam material, which had been installed behind the stage. The foam was of a kind intended for use in packaging and product display and not for sound-treating buildings, and would not *have been treated with fire-retardant materials used in acoustic foam. Witnesses to the fire have reported that once ignited, flames spread across the foam at approximately one foot per second.*

Through attorneys, club owners said they did not give permission to the band to use pyrotechnics. Band members claimed they had permission. In the early days after the fire, there was considerable effort to assign and avoid blame on the part of the band, the nightclub owners, the manufacturers and distributors of the foam material and pyrotechnics, and the concert promoters. On December 9, 2003 Jeffrey A. and Michael A. Derderian, the two owners of The Station nightclub, and Daniel M. Biechele, Great White's former road manager, were charged with 200 counts of involuntary manslaughter — two per death. All three pleaded not guilty to the charges. The Derderians also were fined $1.07 million for failing to carry workers' compensation insurance for their employees, four of whom died in the blaze.

Superior Court Judge Francis J. Darigan sentenced Biechele to 15 years in prison, with four to serve and 11 years suspended, plus three years probation, for his role in setting off the nightclub fire. As jury selection was happening in the second criminal trial of Nightclub owners Jeffrey and Michael Derderian, the Derderians struck a plea bargain with prosecutors that would see Michael Derderian serve four years in a minimum security prison, and Jeffrey Derderian's 10 year sentence would be suspended in return for 500 hours of community service.

From this author's professional standpoint critical errors were made by the security personnel at the Station Club the night of the fire. There are several key points that were overlooked by security personnel. The club owners said they did not give permission to the band to use pyrotechnics. Band members claimed they had permission.

It is the duty of the cooler to ensure that the person in charge of pyrotechnics is licensed and has the appropriate state permit to conduct the said event and that this information is reported to management. In this case the band manager did not have the appropriate license or permits, thus should have been shutdown by the head of security and management -PERIOD. Sprinklers were not installed in The Station, nor would they have been required for such existing structures under 2003 editions of the model codes. A heat detection/fire alarm system was installed in the building and was activated (sound and strobe) by the fire, 41 seconds after the fire started. Thus with this being the case, security needed to have quick access to at least 4 to 6, twenty pound portable fire extinguishers. With Pyrotechnics being used at anytime, the author would have stationed bouncers at both ends of the stage with fire extinguishers in hand. The fire marshal stated that all of the building's four exits were functioning and that most of the bodies were recovered from near the building's front entrance. The fire was "the main contributing factor" to their deaths.

"Human nature being what it is, they tried to go out the same way they came in" and were trapped, He said. "That was the problem." The fire marshal said the other three exits had signs with battery-powered lights, but people couldn't see them. "The reason for the total darkness was the density and the intensity of the smoke that was produced by the burning materials: the panel, the soundproofing, suspended ceiling and so forth,"

Sadly enough, it is obvious that if proper security protocol was followed on this occasion the dreadful catastrophe would never have happened.

PERSONAL IDENTIFICATION

Personal identification in bouncing is critical. It is very important that security personnel where a shirt or ID badge that conveys to all that he/she is employed with the nightclub or bar as a security professional. During altercations or just representing the establishment, it is important that security personnel are recognized and acknowledged as authoritative individuals. For this reason it is this author's professional opinion that the word "SECURITY' be printed in plain site on both the front and back of a security shirt. Some nightclub and bar owners prefer to have their security wear shirts with the word 'STAFF' on the back, consciously thinking that this will give the bouncer a more 'user friendly' overtone. However, in a court of law criminal charges are filed and a verdict handed out regardless of what shirt the bouncer was wearing at the time of the altercation. It is again this author's professional opinion that identification needs to be accurate and factual. It is obvious that among professional organizations accurate identification is very important. Thus, this is why it is against the law to impersonate a law enforcement officer. When a person in the nightclub or bar needs security assistance, they should be able to distinguish this person from other personnel not hired nor trained as a nightclub security professional.

CLOTHING & FOOTWEAR

Clothing should be form fitting and comfortable. You are representing your club so dress with pride. Tank tops, muscle shirts, shirts with cut off sleeves are not proper attire. They present the wrong image for a bouncer. Even worse are security personnel who wear dark sunglasses (at night), baggy clothing, fingerless SAP gloves, half-gloves, carry 2 foot long D-cell battery flashlights, large knives, stun guns, brass knuckles, blackjacks...etc. All this will bring nothing but a lawsuit against the club and yourself. Be a professional and approach the job with the right mindset.

Footwear should be lace up if possible and have a flat sole. Composite Toe protective boots and shoes are always an excellent idea. Cross-trainers, work boots, combat-style boots are very good. Avoid footwear that is loose, has high heels and/or smooth soles. Every doorman/bouncer needs a good quality flashlight. It does not have to be big but it must be easy to carry, durable and project a powerful enough beam. It must be used to not only check ID's and dark corners in the club but also to escort patrons or staff members outside in total darkness.

Laser pointers

Laser pointers are an excellent way of communicating with fellow staff members. In a medium to dark club, the laser pointer can catch the attention of a fellow bouncer or DJ. They can be used to pinpoint trouble and direct other security members to it. Laser pointers should never be directed into the eyes of a person or animal or into any moving vehicle in which the driver or pilot could be distracted.

The output of laser pointers is generally limited to 1 mW or 5 mW in order to prevent accidental damage to the retina of human eyes. Usually, pen lasers are class 2 or class 3a lasers, which require extended viewing times to damage the retina severely. There is some debate about whether outputs of 5 mW may damage eyes if viewed through spectacles or contact lenses. The Food and Drug Administration (FDA) has determined that Class 3a lasers could cause injury to the eye if viewed directly for approximately 0.25 seconds, although it has cited evidence that exposure to visible lasers is "usually" limited by the blink reflex of the eye, which they have timed at just under 0.25 seconds.

In the late 1990s, the laser pointer became a fad amongst adolescents as an irritant to be pointed stealthily at a movie theater screen or even at a person's eyes. During late 2004 a man was arrested in USA under terrorist laws when he was identified as pointing a high power green laser pointer into the cockpit of an airplane.

The USA recently made it a Federal offense, punishable by up to 5 years in prison, to point a laser at an aircraft. Despite legislation limiting the output of laser pointers in some countries (such as the USA and Australia), higher-power devices are currently produced in other regions (especially China and Hong Kong), and are frequently imported by customers who purchase them directly via Internet mail order. The legality of such transactions is not always clear; typically, the lasers are sold as research or OEM devices (which are not subject to the same power restrictions), with a disclaimer that they are not to be used as pointers. Despite the disclaimers, such lasers are frequently sold in packaging resembling that for laser pointers. Lasers of this type may not include safety features sometimes found on laser modules sold for research purposes. As powerful handheld green lasers become more popular in today's market, it has become known that irresponsible use of higher-powered green lasers can be disastrous. Experts say that a direct shot to the eye from a laser over 15 mW can permanently damage the eye within a fraction of a second. The risk becomes greater with more powerful lasers, which are readily available on the Internet today.

Radio Communication Systems

Radio's and earpieces are excellent for security communication. There are many different types on the market. It has come to my attention that Radio Shack sells a variety of affordable radios and a new model throat mic. But there are many things to look out for when looking to invest in a more elaborate noise-canceling headset. You get very much what you pay for and finding the right headset may become a compromise between price and suitability.

Noise canceling mic capsules - These mics take in some of the background noise from the back of the mic and passively cancel it out with any noise picked up from the front of the mic.
In theory when you press the talk switch you are left (mostly) with your voice and without the noise! The result is very much dependant on the capsule. Good mics are generally found on Ear-defending headsets from OTTO, Peltor and TELEX. They are big, expensive but they work. But perhaps not suited to club security work.

Remote speaker mics -These are the mics you will have seen on Law enforcement officers lapels. They are a combined speaker and a microphone with a big PTT on the side. They also have a socket for an earpiece that overrides the speaker output when plugged in. These mics are good in high noise environments because of the way they work. They are insensitive, you have to talk very closely into one to make it pick up - hence there is less background noise. They can be inexpensive but they could be grabbed in a physical altercation.

THROAT MICS- Throat mics work on vibrational pick up rather than air vibration. They will not therefore pick up ambient noise. However buyer beware. Buy your radio to suit the mic. They require a switching voltage to make them work. If your radio does not have the right voltage output they will not perform to their optimum. Further they require the user to find the optimum "sweet position" on their neck for pick-up. At this point the audio output will sound closest to the user's voice. Their weak point is that because they work on vibration they will never sound like the person's voice who is using them. Hold your nose and talk -what you hear is approximately what you will get! Now this time when you talk feel under your Adam's apple with your thumb and index finger either side of it. When you talk you will feel the vibration they will pick-up. You can quickly train yourself to adapt your voice to produce more vibration and less output from your mouth and noise. In theory, they will pick up a whisper, well as we have learned, they don't pick up the whisper but its vibration! Other things that affect their audio quality - How many pick-ups 1 or 2. One only will loose contact when you turn your head. If it has a Non-adjustable neckband the sweet spot can't be reached or you get poor skin contact reducing vibrational transfer to the mic. Very muscular or super size necks do not vibrate so well either. In addition, the radio quality will also affect the overall performance. The more you pay the better the audio clarity in general. Search out low cost alternatives, try them out and assess how much of your requirement they achieve. If it's 80% or more of your requirement then to achieve the final 20% the cost may be inversely proportional to the improvement.

DECT Wireless Belt packs

These are wireless intercom belt packs.

Working at 2.4GHz with digital transmission these system provide the possibility of full duplex communications (being able to transmit as well as receive). The belt packs are lightweight and many provide earpiece style boom mics with noise canceling mic capsules. If and when I use a radio, I too have had problems communicating with others. What I have found works for me, is this. I buy a pair of foam earplugs, placed one of the earplugs in the ear opposite the receiver earpiece, and the other over the mic. I hollow out the earplug that is placed over the mic so that it fits snuggly. One of our guys even made a small deflector and placed it over the outside of the mic. This helps reduce the noise of the club in the background as he is transmitting.

Radios are a great asset for any club. It seems that all security personnel have the same problems with them. You have to turn the volume up so loud to hear that your eardrum can get damaged. Or, you have to shout into the mic just to get a message out.

To maintain good radio etiquette, operators should observe the following guidelines and rules:

1. Keep transmissions as short and direct as possible.

2. Restrict radio traffic to that which is necessary for the safe and efficient operation of the club. No sexual or defamatory remarks of any kind at any time.

3. Begin and end each transmission with an identifier such as a name or a call that is understood by all radio operators in the group.

4. Use the term "over" when ending a transmission and when expecting a response when ever possible.

5. Use the term "out" at the end of a transmission when no response is expected whenever possible.

6. The FCC expressly forbids transmissions of vulgar language and music at any time.

7. The designated radio operator is responsible for any transmissions, regardless of who is talking into the microphone.

8. Do not use the radio for private "chit-chat" or "horseplay". If you want to chat with a friend or an employee, do so in person.

9. In a true emergency, any person is permitted to make an emergency transmission on any frequency.

10. Think before you speak.

The above items are only a few of the things that need to be taken into consideration when operating a two-way radio system. Use good judgment and restraint at all times. The radios are a safety and observation tool only. They are not to be used as a toy. Be professional and considerate of the other team members. This author would like to thank David the Bouncer for this excellent annotation on radio etiquette.

Security Wands

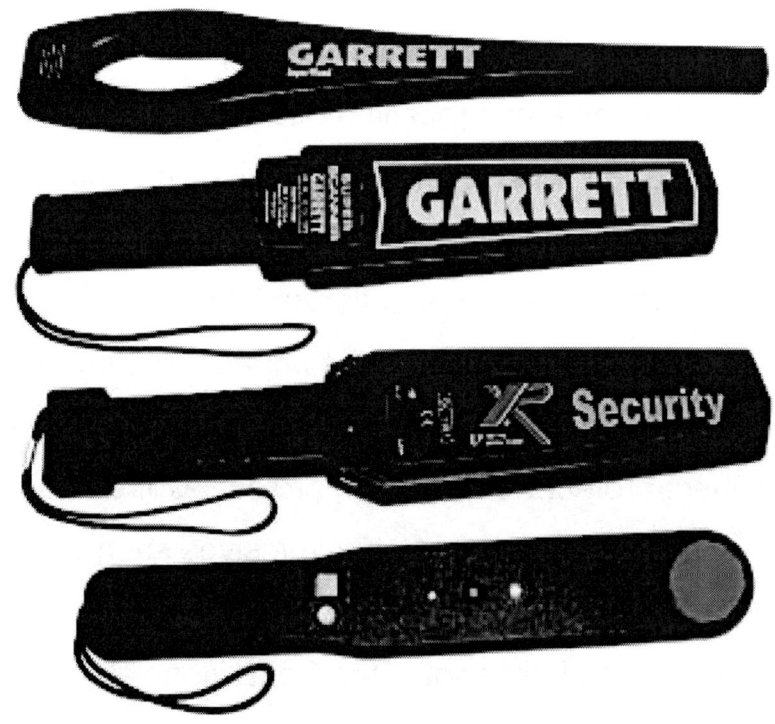

This is a hand held device used to detect metal objects hidden on a person. The wand is turned on and waved just a few inches off the person's body. The wand emits a beeping sound when it detects metal objects. A long-time favorite of security and law enforcement professionals around the world, the Security wand virtually eliminates the need for pat downs during weapon screening, saving patrons from embarrassment and helping to protect security/law enforcement officers from needles and other harmful paraphernalia.

Body Armor

Bulletproof vests are an excellent tool in the trade of nightclub security. Especially in high risk nightclubs where gang violence is common place, or the security professional has received death threats from a potentially violent patron. Also where the bouncer/doorman does protective VIP escorts or makes a money drop after hours at a bank. A ballistic vest, otherwise known as a bulletproof vest or body armor, is a protective torso covering that absorbs the impact from gun-fired projectiles and explosive fragments. Soft vests made from layers of tightly woven fibers protect wearers from projectiles fired from handguns, shotguns and shrapnel from explosives such as hand grenades. When metal or ceramic plates are used with a soft vest, it can also protect wearers from shots fired from rifles.

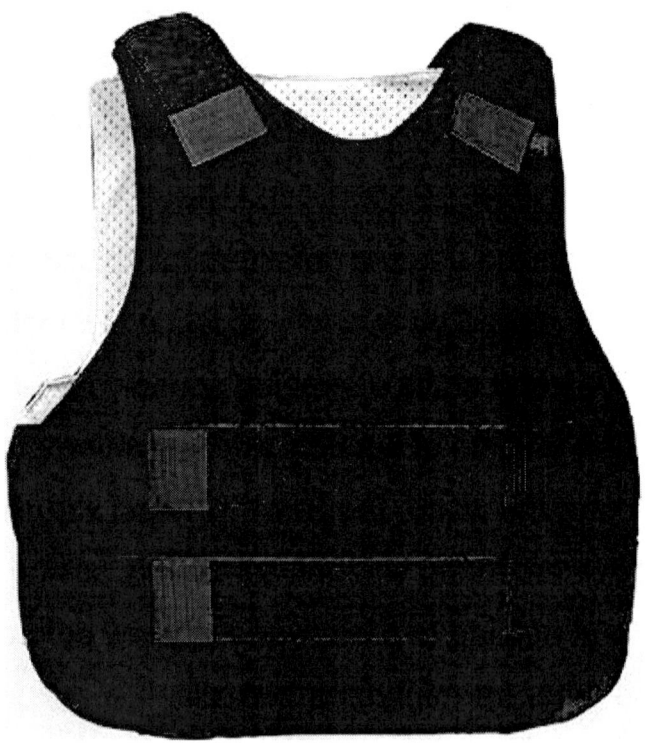

Police forces and private security guards commonly wear soft vests, and hard-plate reinforced vests are worn by combat soldiers in the armies of various nations as well as armed response police forces. The term "bullet-proof" is a ambiguous since these vests, depending on the armor level (see below) may provide little or no protection against rifle ammunition or even against handgun ammunition fired from a pistol-caliber carbine.

The exception is the common .22 LR ammunition, which can usually be stopped by these vests even when fired from a rifle. These vests are usually protective against handgun ammunition fired from handguns, depending on the armor level of the vest. Vests may be augmented with metal (steel or titanium), ceramic or polyethylene plates that provide extra protection to vital areas. These hard armor plates have proven effective against all handgun bullets and a range of rifles. These "tactical body armor" vests have become standard in military use, as soft body armor vests are ineffective against most military rifle rounds. The CRISAT NATO (Collaborative Research Into Small Arms Technology-North Atlantic Treaty Organization) standard for body armor specifies the use of titanium backing. This titanium plate may be removable or sewn in.

A vest does not protect the wearer by deflecting bullets. Instead, the layers of material catch the bullet and spread its force over a larger portion of the body, absorbing energy more quickly and hopefully bringing it to a stop before it can penetrate into the body. This tends to deform the bullet, further reducing its ability to penetrate. While a vest can prevent bullet wounds, the wearer still absorbs the bullet's energy, which can cause blunt force trauma. The majority of users experience only bruising, but impacts can still cause severe internal injuries.

Most vests offer little protection against arrows, ice picks, stabbing knife blows, bullets with their points sharpened or armor-piercing rounds. As the force is concentrated in a relatively small area with bladed weapons and armor-piercing rounds, they can push through the weave of most bullet-resistant fabrics. Specially designed vests that protect against bladed weapons and sharp objects are often used in vests for prison guards and other law enforcement officers. Some materials like Dyneema offer considerable protection against bladed weapons and slash attacks.

Performance standards

Both the Underwriters Laboratories (UL Standard 752) and the United States National Institute of Justice (NIJ Standard 0101.04) have specific performance standards for bullet resistant vests used by law enforcement. The US NIJ rates vests on the following scale against penetration and also blunt trauma protection (deformation) (Table from NIJ Standard 0101.04):

Armor Level	Protects Against
Type I (.22 LR; .380 ACP)	This armor protects against .22 caliber Long Rifle Lead Round Nose (LR LRN) bullets, with nominal masses of 2.6 g (40 gr) at a reference velocity of 329 m/s (1080 ft/s ± 30 ft/s) and .380 ACP Full Metal Jacketed Round Nose (FMJ RN) bullets, with nominal masses of 6.2 g (95 gr) at a reference velocity of 322 m/s (1055 ft/s ± 30 ft/s).
Type IIA (9 mm; .40 S&W)	This armor protects against 9 mm Full Metal Jacketed Round Nose (FMJ RN) bullets, with nominal masses of 8.0 g (124 gr) at a reference velocity of 341 m/s (1120 ft/s ± 30 ft/s) and .40 S&W caliber Full Metal Jacketed (FMJ) bullets, with nominal masses of 11.7 g (180 gr) at a reference velocity of 322 m/s (1055 ft/s ± 30 ft/s). It also provides protection against the threats mentioned in [Type I].
Type II (9 mm; .357 Magnum)	This armor protects against 9 mm Full Metal Jacketed Round Nose (FMJ RN) bullets, with nominal masses of 8.0 g (124 gr) at a reference velocity of 367 m/s (1205 ft/s ± 30 ft/s) and 357 Magnum Jacketed Soft Point (JSP) bullets, with nominal masses of 10.2 g (158 gr) at a reference velocity of 436 m/s (1430 ft/s ± 30 ft/s). It also provides protection against the threats mentioned in [Types I and IIA].
Type IIIA (High Velocity 9 mm; .44 Magnum)	This armor protects against 9 mm Full Metal Jacketed Round Nose (FMJ RN) bullets, with nominal masses of 8.0 g (124 gr) at a reference velocity of 436 m/s (1430 ft/s ± 30 ft/s) and .44 Magnum Semi Jacketed Hollow Point (SJHP) bullets, with nominal masses of 15.6 g (240 gr) at a reference velocity of 436 m/s (1430 ft/s ± 30 ft/s). It also provides protection against most handgun threats.
Type III (Rifles)	This armor protects against 7.62 mm Full Metal Jacketed (FMJ) bullets (U.S. Military designation M80), with nominal masses of 9.6 g (148 gr) at a reference velocity of 847 m/s (2780 ft/s ± 30 ft/s) or less. It also

Type IV (Armor Piercing Rifle)	**provides protection against the threats mentioned in [Types I, IIA, II, and IIIA].**
	This armor protects against .30 caliber armor piercing (AP) bullets (U.S. Military designation M2 AP), with nominal masses of 10.8 g (166 gr) at a reference velocity of 878 m/s (2880 ft/s ± 30 ft/s). It also provides at least single hit protection against the threats mentioned in [Types I, IIA, II, IIIA, and III].

Bomb disposal officers often wear heavy armor designed to protect against most effects of a moderate sized explosion, such as bombs encountered in terror threats. Full head helmet, covering the face and some degree of protection for limbs is mandatory in addition to very strong armor for the torso. An insert to protect the spine is usually applied to the back, in case an explosion blasts the wearer. Visibility, and mobility of the wearer may be severely limited. In terms of Kevlar, a IIA vest has around sixteen layers and a IIIA vest around thirty layers. German standards allow for bullet impact depression of 20 millimeters on the mannequin's wax body under the vest; US standards allow for more than twice that (44 millimeters), which can be potentially lethal. In addition, there are vests available for police dogs that offer a measure of protection for the animals.

An Aramid vest's material must not get wet, because it will lose its protective capability until dry again, or in some cases be permanently degraded (water acts as a lubricant, helping the bullet slip through between the fibers; it may also weaken the structure of the fiber by breaking hydrogen bonds, see Kevlar for details).

Most bulletproof vests have panels in sealed enclosures, but waterproofing is usually not perfect. Dyneema and Spectra based vests do not have the same difficulties with water.

Legality

Body armor is legal in most countries. One exception is Australia, where body armor has been prohibited for some time. This ban may have its origins in the late 19th century, when the iconic Australian outlaw and folk hero Ned Kelly used homemade armor with mixed results. While the steel armor worn by Kelly defeated the soft lead, low velocity bullets fired by police Martini-Henry rifles, it greatly restricted his movement. United States law restricts possession of body armor for convicted violent felons. Many US states also have penalties for possession or use of body armor by felons. In February of 1999, the late Russell Jones a.k.a. "Ol' Dirty Bastard", was arrested in California for possession of body armor by a convicted felon. In other states, such as Kentucky, they do not prohibit possession, but deny probation or parole for a person convicted of certain violent crimes while wearing body armor and carrying a deadly weapon. Canadian legislation makes it legal to wear and to purchase body armor such as ballistic vests. However, there are current proposals to the legislation to make it illegal to wear such body armor during the commission of a criminal offense. In Germany, body armor is illegal because it is classified as a passive weapon.

Tactical Batons

*This author has been an ASP Expandable Baton / Monadnock MEB Baton Instructor and a Certified Ocat Pepper Spray Instructor for 5 years. I am a strong advocate in the art of Tactical Baton and OC pepper spray training. It is this author's belief that the use of such equipment in nightclub security will actually discourage unruly patrons from wanting to fight with security staff and it safe guards both the patron and the security professional.

My hypothesis is based on the four following factors:

1. The unruly patron has an obvious disadvantage in actual fight.

2. The psychological advantage of the security professional possessing a Tactical Baton and Pepper Spray is the visual representation of authority and control.

3. The violent patron will come to the realization that the security team will not accommodate his aggressive behavior by fighting him in a manner that will boost his ego or allow him to show off.

4. The unruly patron will have no choice but to keep the level of negative behavior at a verbal standpoint avoiding the obvious outcome should he decide to take the dispute to a physical level. This gives the bouncer/security the opportunity to use verbal de-escalation techniques to make progress toward a Win-Win situation.

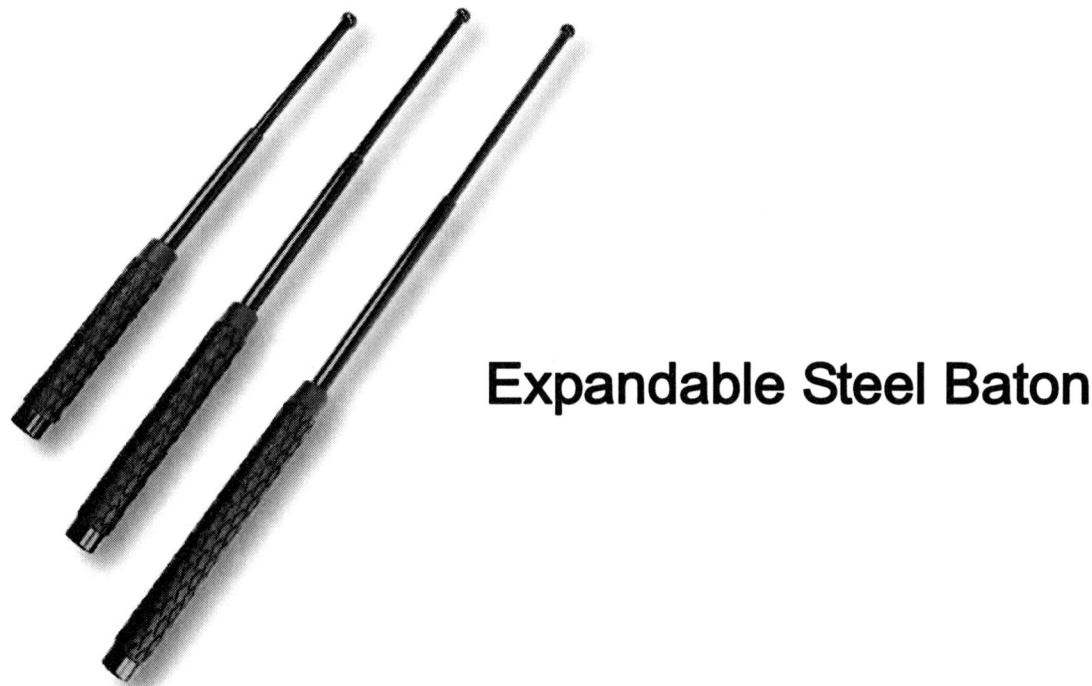

Expandable Steel Baton

The MEB® programs have evolved from mid-1985 to what it has become today, the worlds leading straight and expandable baton program. This author is a trained instructor of the MEB program and the PPCT Shockwave system, which are designed to teach qualified police officers and other security personnel techniques to defend themselves and others from harm, as well as teaching a baton-assisted arm lock for controlling non-compliant subjects. When purchasing a Tactical Baton make sure to buy a high-quality baton like a Monadock or ASP. Cheaper made batons will bend, break and lockup. Your life depends on not only your ability but also your equipment. **A professional uses professional equipment.**

*This author strongly recommends that this devise be used only if the doorman has been properly trained and certified to do so with permission from the establishment and local Law Enforcement.

OC Pepper spray

Pepper spray (also known as OC spray (from "Oleoresin Capsicum"), OC gas, capsicum spray, or oleoresin capsicum) is a lachrymatory agent (a chemical compound that irritates the eyes to cause tears, pain, and even temporary blindness) that is used in riot control, crowd control and personal self-defense including defense against dogs and bears. It is a non-lethal agent that can be deadly in rare cases. The American Civil Liberties Union claims to have documented fourteen fatalities from the use of pepper spray. The active ingredient in pepper spray is capsaicin, which is a chemical derived from the fruit of plants in the Capsicum genus, including chilies. Long-term effects of pepper spray have not been effectively researched.

The HPLC (High Performance Liquid Chromatography) method is used to measure the amount of capsaicin within pepper sprays. Scoville Heat Units (SHU) are used to measure the hotness of pepper spray. A synthetic analogue of capsaicin, pelargonic acid vanillylamide (desmethyldihydrocapsaicin), is used in another version of pepper spray known as PAVA spray that is used in England. Another synthetic counterpart of pepper spray, pelargonic acid morpholide, was developed and is widely used in Russia. Its effectiveness compared to natural pepper spray is unclear and it has caused some injuries. Pepper spray typically comes in canisters, which are often small enough to be carried or concealed in a pocket or purse. Pepper spray can also be bought concealed in items such as rings, pens and pagers. There are also Pepper-Spray projectiles available, which can be fired from a paintball gun.

Mace vs. Pepper Spray

Don't get Mace confused with Pepper Spray. Mace is an irritant that is very similar to tear gas, unlike pepper spray which is an inflammatory agent. Pepper spray will have an effect on those that feel no pain, such as those under the influence of drugs or alcohol. Mace may or may not have an effect on these types. Unlike Pepper Spray, Mace will NOT cause inflammation of the capillaries causing temporary blindness, nausea, cut off all but life support breathing, and create a very strong burning or stinging sensation. It is important to note that Mace is also a brand name.

Effects

Pepper spray is an inflammatory agent, not an irritant like Mace. It causes immediate closing of the eyes, runny nose, difficulty breathing and coughing. The length of the effects depends on the strength of the spray but the average full effect lasts around thirty to forty-five minutes, with mitigated effects lasting for hours. The Journal of Investigative Ophthalmology and Visual Science published a study that concluded that single exposure of the eye to OC is harmless, but repeated exposure can result in long-lasting changes in corneal sensitivity. They found no lasting decrease in visual acuity. The European Parliament Scientific and Technological Options Assessment (STOA) published in 1998 "An Appraisal of Technologies of Political Control" with extensive information on pepper spray and tear gas. They write:

"*The effects of Pepper Spray are far more severe, including temporary blindness, which last from 15-30 minutes, a burning sensation of the skin, which last from 45 to 60 minutes, upper body spasms, which force a person to bend forward, and uncontrollable coughing, making it difficult to breathe or speak for between 3 to 15 minutes.*"

*For those with asthma, taking other drugs, or subject to restraining techniques that restrict the breathing passages, there is a risk of death.

The Los Angeles Times has reported at least 61 deaths associated with police use of pepper spray since 1990 in the USA, and the American Civil Liberties Union (ACLU) documented 27 deaths in custody of people sprayed with Pepper Spray in California alone, since 1993.The US Army concluded in a 1993 Aberdeen Proving Ground study that pepper spray could cause "Mutagenic effects, carcinogenic effects, sensitization, cardiovascular and pulmonary toxicity, neurotoxicity, as well as possible human fatalities. There is a risk in using this product on a large and varied population". However, the pepper spray got the go ahead despite the reservations of the US military scientists after FBI tests gave it the all clear. It has subsequently been revealed that the head of the FBI's Less-Than lethal Weapons Program, Special Agent Thomas W. W. Ward, took a $57,000 bribe from a pepper gas manufacturer to give the Zarc product Capstun, the all clear."

Deactivation and first aid

Though there is no way of completely neutralizing pepper spray, its effect can be minimized or stopped. As veteran chili eaters know, capsaicin is not soluble in water, and even large volumes of water will have little to no effect. It is, however, soluble in fats and oils, so milk or detergents can be used to blunt its effects and wash it off. North American street medics use a non-toxic eye drop solution of 1:1 water and aluminum hydroxide (Maalox) which helps neutralize pepper spray and relieve symptoms.

Victims should be encouraged to blink vigorously in order to encourage tears, which will help flush the irritant from the eyes.

Some of the oil can be washed off the face using a degreasing, non-oily soap such as a mild dish detergent, and a fan will provide some relief. Some "triple-action" pepper sprays also contain "tear gas" (CS gas), which can be neutralized with sodium metabisulfite (Campden tablets, used in homebrewing), though it, too, is fat-soluble and could be washed off to a degree with milk, and some contain a UV "blanketing" dye (little can be done against this, but its effects are not nearly as dramatic).

Legality

Laws on Pepper Spray in the United States of America differ between states. Using pepper spray irresponsibly can incur criminal or civil liability regardless if you are certified to carry or not. Spraying an innocent victim in the face can be a crime. Much like a punch in the face, it would be charged as assault or battery in most jurisdictions. The justification for using pepper sprays must either be self-defense from personal injury or an arrest situation, and the force must be reasonable under the circumstances. For example, the law says you cannot lawfully spray someone in the face for using obscene language or because they look intimidating.

* You cannot buy pepper spray by mail or through the Internet from Hawaii, Indiana, Massachusetts, Michigan, New Jersey, New York, Pennsylvania, Rhode Island, and Wisconsin.

Washington, D.C.: possession of Pepper Spray must be registered with the DC Metropolitan Police.

Massachusetts: Pepper Spray can only be sold to holders of firearm identification cards

New York: licensed firearms dealers or pharmacists may only sell Pepper Spray.

Wisconsin: Pepper Spray is limited to containers of 15-60 grams of 10% active ingredient without dyes or CN/CS.

Michigan: Pepper Spray is legal if it has less than 2% of the active ingredient, this decreases the length of the effects but not the SHU. Sprays containing a mixture of CN/CS are also banned. Otherwise Pepper Spray is an over the counter purchase.
In many (but not all) other states, Pepper Spray can be purchased at various stores and carried legally by anyone over 18.

* Internationally pepper spray is banned for use in war by the 1972 Biological Weapons convention but not for internal security use.

In **Australia** it is classified as a prohibited weapon, and it is illegal for anyone other than police officers to carry a capsicum spray.

In **Canada** it is classified as a prohibited weapon. A number of dog, and significantly stronger bear pepper sprays are legal to own. However, use of these items against humans will most likely result in the user being prosecuted.

In **Denmark** possession of pepper spray is illegal for private citizens, but a trial period is currently in effect, where police officers in most metropolitan areas carry pepper spray as part of their standard equipment. This trial period has been initiated following the shooting (and often killing) of a number of mentally ill citizens who have behaved violently, or in a threatening manner, leaving the police force in want of a defensive, non-lethal weapon.

In **Finland** it is classified as a device governed by the "Firearm Act", and possession of pepper spray requires a license. Licenses are issued for defensive purposes and to individuals working job where such a device is needed such as the private security sector. Government organizations such as defense forces and police are exempt. Concentrations are also limited to 5% active ingredient in OC sprays and 2%/2% in combinations sprays such as CN/OC.

In **Germany** privately owned pepper spray may fall into two different categories. Sprays that bear the test mark of the Materialprüfungsanstalt may be owned and carried solely for the purpose of defense against animals. Such sprays are not legally considered as weapons. Sprays that do not bear this test mark are classified as prohibited weapons. It is nevertheless strictly prohibited to carry pepper spray at (or on the way to and from) demonstrations - whether it bears a test mark or not.

In **Hong Kong** Pepper Spray is classified as "arms" under HK Laws. Chapter 238 "FIREARMS AND AMMUNITION ORDINANCE", without a valid license from the Hong Kong Police Force, it is a crime and can result a fine of $100,000 and to imprisonment for 14 years.

In **Italy** OC it is considered a self-defense weapon and it is legal to own it when the active principle is less than 10%. Spray made with CS is illegal.

In **Latvia** pepper spray is classified as a self-defense weapon, and it is available to anyone over 16. Anyone over 18 can buy gas pistol loaded with pepper or tear gas cartridges for self-defense.

In the **Netherlands** it is classified as a prohibited weapon, and it is illegal for anyone other than police officers to carry a capsicum spray.

In **Norway** real pepper spray is only used by the police. The publicly available defense spray often called pepper spray is actually based on isopropyl alcohol.

In **Poland** pepper spray is not classified as a weapon, so it is available to anyone over 18.

In **Russia** pepper spray is a fully legal self-defense weapon and can be bought without license by any person over the age of 18 (passport being required for purchase). Its effect on animals is advertised as additional feature, compared with tear gas sprays. Law prohibits carrying it at demonstrations.

In **South Africa** it is not a licensed product and is freely available as an over the counter security product. Generally carried and used by private security officers and armed reaction officers as well as police and members of the public. A pepper spray projectile is also available also without license. Anyone using pepper spray as anything but a defensive weapon can still be charged with a firearms .

In **Sweden** it is classified as an offensive weapon and possession of pepper spray requires a license. However, as of 2006, no such license has been issued.

In **Spain** approved pepper spray made with 5% CS is available to anyone over 18.

In the **United Kingdom**, "Any weapon of whatever description designed or adapted for the discharge of any noxious liquid, gas or other thing" is classed as a section 5 firearm (Firearms Act 1968). The same act covers other prohibited weapons such as automatic firearms and rocket launchers, all of which can only be possessed by permission of the Home Secretary. Although legal for police officers, recent debates have arisen whether such a weapon should be legal for civilians as means of defensive purposes only. At present a number of legal alternative dye sprays are sold in the UK that have the effect of temporarily blinding the attacker but do not constitute noxious substances and so do not contravene this act.

How to Test Your OC Canister for Pressure

If you wish to test your canister for pressure, make your spray burst only one second and do not do this often, as there may be as little as twenty seconds or less worth of spray in some models. The label or instructions of a good brand should tell you how many seconds of spray it has. Shake the canister to determine the quantity of ingredients left inside it. Canisters may have a shelf life of three to six years, but they are usually conservatively dated to expire in one year. Always shake the canister prior to use. Pepper spray canisters have the active ingredient mixed in a liquid and a pressurized gas propellant.

Although the spray life is indefinite, it does start to lose 'Pressure' over time. Any use of the spray beyond the expiration date is highly unadvisable. **We strongly advise you to replace your pepper spray every year!** That way you are always assured of the pressure and potency of the spray. If you do end up in a dangerous situation, remember that your number one priority is not to fight, but seek control and diversion. Brandishing your pepper spray at a violent patron (if he isn't aiming a gun at you) may be all that is needed to allowed you to maintain control of the situation or make the person leave without an incident. If you have to use your pepper spray make sure you have at least four feet of distance between you and the threat. Aim the spray at the eyes and facial region of the threat then release a 1 to 2 second burst of spray. After you have done this MOVE out of the way clear of the OC sprayed area, but keep your eyes on the threat. Pepper spray ingredients can take a couple of moments to cause a reaction and by watching the reactions of the threat you will be able to determine if the threat will require another shot of pepper spray.

*This author recommends that all security personnel take a course in OC Pepper Spray proficiency and be come certified. I instill in all my students the acute message:

> **"With Great Power…Comes Great Responsibility."**

* NOTE : This devise can be used only if the doorman has been properly trained and certified to do so with permission from the establishment and local Law Enforcement.

The following newspaper report is a testament to my teachings.

E2 (nightclub)

The Epitome Chicago and its upstairs dance floor E2 were a popular nightclub in Chicago until on the night of Monday, February 17, 2003, a stampede occurred in which 21 people were killed and more than 50 injured. The proximate cause of the stampede was reported to be that security used pepper spray to break up a fight. Both because of the noxious spray and also because of panic among those who were unsure what the chemical was, many patrons made a rush towards the exits. The cause of death was not fire, as in the case of many other famous nightclub disasters, but trampling and suffocation. Although a security guard opened at least one emergency exit, there were disputed reports of one chained shut. The only exit known to most patrons was the narrow, steep front stairwell, with narrow doors that opened inward, against fire code. The doors at the top opened outward, and as the crowd pushed them open, people standing on the small upper landing were tossed down the stairs.

The doors, normally open, were closed after security guards removed the participants in a fight. As more patrons tried to exit, they were forced on top of the bodies of those who had already fallen. Security guards attempted to remove bodies from below, but the pile of people grew faster than they could clear it. Captured in shocking photographs and news footage, dozens of people crammed in narrow exits: they were stacked one on top of the other, unable to move and, in many cases, even breathe. [Sadovi: 2007b]

More than 1,500 stampeded in an attempt to escape the spray and chaos inside. (Wilgoren: 2003a) There were a number of controversies associated with this case. Many alleged that the club owners consistently violated building codes on the number of patrons who could be present. Jesse Jackson had in the past supported the club owners when community groups had sought to shut the club down for building code and other violations. (Wilgoren: 2003b) There were allegations that the security staff was improperly trained. At least one member of the security staff was reported to have used pepper spray to stop a fight between two patrons. [Sandvovi: 2007a] .

WEIGHT TRAINING AND SELF-DEFENSE

It is very important in the trade of Nightclub Security that the Bouncer/Doorman stays in good shape both mentally and physically. One cannot build a strong house on a weak foundation, thus the importance of strength, power, and endurance. Better performance can be the result of a number of factors. This effect is primarily the outcome of efficient technique, development of speed, endurance, strength and a mature competitive attitude. The development of all round strength is best achieved via circuit training and then progressing this through weight training. This author recommends joining a reputable gym that has good trainers. This author was an amateur powerlifter back in the mid-80's and found powerlifting to be a great training system. Powerlifting is a sport that was conceived as a pure test of strength. Powerlifting is of relatively modern origin, with the first formal competitions occurring in the mid 1960s. Powerlifting comprises three lifts: the Squat, Bench Press, and Deadlift. Powerlifting competitions may be comprised of one, two or all three of the lifting disciplines. Athletes are categorized by sex, age and bodyweight. Each competitor is allowed three attempts at each lift, the best lift in each discipline being added to their total. The lifter with the highest total is the winner. In cases where two or more lifters achieve the same total, the person with the lightest bodyweight wins.

*Prior to starting any training program, this author recommends you have a medical examination to ensure it is safe for you to do so. Any application of this training program is at the athlete's own discretion and risk.

The following is a selection of exercises that should be included in a general strength-training program.

- Military Shoulder Press
- Bench Press
- Lat Pull downs
- Seated rows
- Triceps Extensions
- Calf Raise
- Biceps Curls
- Forearm curls
- Leg Curls
- Leg Extension
- Leg Press
- Squats
- Deadlifts

* Use free weights as much as possible. Machines are best used with and after the free weight exercise, to safely exhaust the muscle and get the burn.

An Example of this author's weekly training program

- Monday – work Chest, Back & Shoulders = 3 sets (each) 8-10 Reps.
- Tuesday – work Legs & Arms = 3 sets (each) 8-10 Reps
- Wednesday- Abs & Cardio
- Thursday – work Chest, Back & Shoulders = 3 sets (each) 8-10 Reps.
- Friday – work Legs & Arms = 3 sets (each) 8-10 Reps

 * Allow 3 to 5 minutes recovery between each set and exercise. Weekends off.

Unarmed Self-defense

Unarmed Self-defense comes in many forms. It is this author's philosophical belief that:

"A Martial Art is only as good….as the man who masters it."

Thus it is this author's conjecture that the Martial Art picks the master and not the latter. Today it is not difficult to see the direction that unarmed combat is going. UFC is extremely popular and it's MMA (Mixed Martial Arts) fighting systems are the best in the world. Even the U.S. Navy SEAL's and Ranger Special Forces employ civilian MMA instructors to train their soldiers. This author has witnessed a medium built, 5' 6" - 165lb man with seriously clover-leafed ears (a tell tale sign of a MMA combatant) take a large, 6' 4" - 240lb man outside in the parking lot and defeat him in hand to hand combat in a matter of minutes and some times seconds!The UFC was started as a tournament to find the world's best fighters no matter what their style and was based upon Brazilian Vale Tudo fighting. Although there were a limited number of rules, the UFC was initially known as no holds barred fighting, thus contests were often violent and brutal. Early UFC fights were less sport than spectacle, which led to accusations of brutality and "human cockfighting" by opponents. Political pressures eventually led the UFC into the underground, as pay-per-view providers removed UFC programming, nearly extinguishing the UFC's public visibility. As political pressure mounted, the UFC reformed itself, slowly embracing stricter rules, becoming sanctioned by athletic commissions, and marketing itself as a legitimate sporting event. Dropping the no holds barred label and carrying the banner of mixed martial arts, the UFC has emerged from its political isolation to become more socially acceptable, regaining its position in pay-per-view television. With a cable television deal and legalization of MMA in California, the UFC is currently undergoing a remarkable surge in popularity, along with heightened media coverage.

The Octagon

The UFC uses an octagonal caged enclosure, "The Octagon", to stage bouts. Originally, SEG had trademarked The Octagon and prevented other mixed martial arts promotions from using the same type of cage, but in 2001, Zuffa gave their permission for other promotions to use octagonal cages (while reserving use of the name "Octagon"). Their rationale was that the young sport needed uniformity in order to continue to win official sanctioning. The cage is composed of an eight-sided metal fencing coated with black vinyl, with a diameter of 11.5 m (38 ft), allowing 9 m (30 ft) of space from point to point. The fencing is 1.83 m (6 ft) high. The cage sits on top of a platform, raising it 1.2 m (4 ft) from the ground. It has foam padding around the top of the fencing and between each of the eight sections. It also has two entry-exit gates opposite each other. The mat, painted with sponsorship logos and art, is replaced for each event. All competitors must fight in approved shorts, without shoes or any other sort of foot padding. Shirts, gi's or long pants (including gi pants) are not allowed. Fighters must use approved light gloves (110 to 170 g / 4 to 6 ounces) that allow fingers to grab. These gloves enable fighters to use tremendous punching power with less risk of an injured or broken hand.

Originally the attire for UFC was very open if controlled at all. Many fighters still chose to wear tight-fitting shorts or boxing-type trunks, while others wore long pants or tight wrestling suits.

Multi-tournament champion Royce Gracie wore a Jujutsugi in all his early appearances in UFC. It is this author's professional opinion that a person proficient in both a grappling/wrestling art combined with a hand/leg striking art would be very hard to defeat. "Jui Jutsu" type ground techniques combined with the 'on your feet' -striking style "Muay Thai" is no doubt the ultimate combination. Thus this author recommends that a nightclub security professional find a reputable, highly-recommend school that teaches MMA system or a combination of Jiu Jitsu and Muay Thai fighting styles.

Jiu Jitsu

Canadian Ari 'Boomer' Bolden is a student of this author in the subject of nightclub and bar security but in the art of Jiu Jitsu, Ari is the teacher! An accomplished professional in nightclub security, Ari has been a martial arts practitioner for 20 years and holds black belt rankings in the arts of Jiu Jitsu and Aikido. He currently teaches Jiu Jitsu at his school, the Bujitsu Academy of Victoria.

Jujutsi (Jiu-Jitsu, JuJitsu, Ju-Jitsu) is a martial art that originated in Japan well over 1000 years ago. It was developed to aid the Samurai in unarmed combat, should they be without their weapons on the battlefield. The literal translation of the word 'Jiu-Jitsu' means "Pliable (gentle or flexible) Fighting Art". In other words, it has the ability to apply its techniques depending on what type of attack it encounters. While Jiu-Jitsu practitioners are known to excel in grappling based combat (grabs, holds, and throws), the art can also include: sweeps, joint locks, submissions, arresting techniques, chokes, cranks, strikes, pressure point attacks and even weapons work. It is one of the worlds most sought after and complete martial art form.

There are many styles of Jiu-Jitsu, each with its own focus. These may include styles like: Gracie Jiu-Jitsu (BJJ), Daito Ryu, Fusen Ryu, Goshin, Small Circle, Danzan Ryu, Hakko Ryu or any other type out there today.

Muay Thai

When it comes to this author's Muay Thai training, it is with great pride that I leave this area of expertise to another apprentice of mine. My stepson Brian Allen. Brian is not only a first-rate bouncer, but one of the finest ex-professional Thai fighter in America. In the early 1990's he was a pioneer of Muay Thai here in the United States. Brian fought as an amateur and studied Muay Thai in Holland, Netherlands before turning pro. Retired now, from competition, Brian still teaches and offers private instruction. I would like to thank Brian for his expert counsel and input in regards to this section.

Muay Thai also known as Thai Boxing or The Art of the Eight Limbs. Muay Thai is a form of marital art practiced in several Southeast Asian countries including Thailand. It is known as Pradal Serey in Cambodia, Tomoi in Malaysia, Muay Lao in Laos. and as a similar style called Lethwei in Myanmar. The different styles of kickboxing in Southeast Asia are analogous to the different types of Kung Fu in China or Silat in the Malay Archipelago. The Thai military uses a modified form of Muay Thai called 'Lerdrit'. Muay Thai has a long history in Thailand and is the country's national sport.

Traditional Muay Thai practiced today, varies slightly from the ancient art Muay Boran and uses kicks and punches in a ring with gloves similar to those used in Western boxing. Muay Thai is referred to as "The Science of Eight Limbs", as the hands, shins, elbows, and knees are all used extensively in this art. A master practitioner of Muay Thai has the ability to execute strikes using eight "points of contact," as opposed to "two points" (fists) in Western boxing and "four points" (fists, feet) used in the primarily sport-oriented forms of martial arts. The basic offensive techniques in Muay Thai use fists, elbows, shins, feet, and knees to strike the opponent.

To bind the opponent for both offensive and defensive moves, stand-up grappling techniques are implemented. This is referred to as 'clinching'. Muay Thai is often a fighting art of attrition, where opponents exchange blows with one another. This is certainly the case with traditional stylists in Thailand, but is a less popular form of fighting in the contemporary world fighting circuit. With the success of Muay Thai in mixed martial arts fighting, it has become the de facto martial art of choice for competitive stand-up fighters. As a result, it has evolved accordingly and incorporated much more powerful hand striking techniques used in western style boxing. Thus, the Thai style of exchanging blow for blow is no longer favorable.

It should be noted that when Muay Thai fighters compete against fighters of other styles (and if the rules permit it), they almost invariably emphasize elbow (sok) and knee (kao) techniques to gain a distinct advantage in fighting. Almost all techniques in Muay Thai use the entire body movement, rotating the body and hip with each kick, punch, and block is what sets Muay Thai apart from the other styles of martial arts.

Like most martial arts, Muay Thai is not without its legendary hero's - Nai Khanom Tom was a famous practitioner of Muay Thai. Around 1774, he was captured along with other Thai prisoners, either in a skirmish or at the fall of the ancient capital of Siam of Ayutthaya.

He was brought to Rangoon in Burma, where the Burmese King Mangra was holding a religious festival in honor of Buddha's relics. The festivities included many forms of entertainment. King Mangra was reported to be curious to see how the various fighting styles of Burma and other countries would compare. At one point, he wanted to see how Muay Boran would compare to the Burmese art Lethwei. Nai Khanomtom was selected to fight against the Burmese champion. Nai Khanomtom did a Wai Kru pre-fight dance that puzzled all of the Burmese. When the fight began, he charged out using punches, kicks, elbows, and knees, quickly pummeled the Burmese opponent. The referee was reported to have stated that the Burmese opponent was distracted by the Wai Kru, so the knockout was invalid. The King then asked if Nai Khanomtom would fight nine other Burmese champions to prove himself. He agreed and fought them all, one after the other with no rest periods between fights. The last Burmese was reputed to be a great boxing teacher. Nai Khanomtom defeated them all in superior fashion. King Mangra was so impressed that he remarked :

"Every part of the Thai is blessed with venom. Even with his bare hands, he can defeat nine or ten opponents. As his lord master was incompetent, the country was lost to the enemy. If his lord had been any good, there was no way the City of Ayutthaya would ever have fallen."

He granted Nai Khanomtom freedom along with the choice of riches or two beautiful Burmese wives. Nai Khanomtom chose the wives as he said that money was easier to find. He then departed with his wives for Siam. Other variations of this story had him also winning the release of his fellow Thai prisoners. His feat is celebrated every March 17 as "Boxer's Day" or "National Muay Thai Day" in his honor and that of Muay Thai's.

Today, some have wrongly attributed the legend of "Nai Khanomtom" to the King Naresuan, who was also once taken by the Burmeses.

THE ART OF THE 4 P's –
' THE PROTECTION OF PATRONS, PERSONNEL & PROPERTY'

Any rational person can understand that in some cases there are violent people who will not de-escalate and listen to reason. Some individuals are just biologically aggressive and find some morbid enjoyment in physical violence. Nothing a bouncer/doorman can say will stop their aggressive behavior. Thus, a nightclub security professional if physically attacked, or if another person is brutality attacked, must use force to stop the attacker. This author, like many other professionals in the trade will not standby and watch a violent patron attack and injure another person. **It is our legal right to use the necessary amount of force needed to protect ourselves and others.** The fact is how can you call the police when you are being punched and kicked!!

The bottom line is: When a situation becomes physically violent the time for talk is over and it is time for the nightclub professional to administer the SAR Matrix appropriate level of force.

Personal protection (or self defense) is a subject that all nightclub security personnel should know something about. While high-quality customer service skills are must in the nightclub hospitality industry, the job of the nightclub bouncer/doorman does require physical intervention from time to time. This may include:

- Restraints
- Arresting tactics
- Takedowns
- Team cooperation
- Breaking up physical altercations
- Self defense

The following information is provided by Ari Bolden an expert in the field of self-defense and nightclub security.

This section is designed to highlight the best tactics and skills in regards to nightclub security. It is not a section on how to become a great street fighter or Ultimate Fighting Champion. **Do not confuse ring competition with real life confrontation.** There is a huge difference between the two. Absolutely no book on the market today will give you the skills you need to become the next world mix martial arts champion. There are only two things that will give you the fighting edge when it comes to self-protection: Training and real world experience.

Remember, the bouncer/doorman is a customer service representative of the establishment and should be as cordial as possible. However, also remember that the primary "job" of a bouncer/doorman is to protect the establishment, the patrons and the staff from potential hazards and dangers. The profession of a bouncer/doorman can be a dangerous one. The goal of this book is to provide the best material possible to protect yourself and others from harm in a nightclub or bar. We have provided the "cold hard facts" of physical intervention in regards to the profession. With over 50 years of nightclub and bar security experience between the author and technical advisers, we hope you will listen to what we have to say.

REALITY VS FANTASY

Real world violence and physical intervention is dynamic, fluid and chaotic. This means that anything can happen in a real fight. The majority of physical altercations will involve people who are intoxicated to some degree. This means that their mental state, physical capabilities (including pain tolerance) may be altered dramatically. Here are some points on the reality of violence in the nightclub business:

- Bar fights and real physical altercations usually last less than 10 seconds.
- There is no tapping out or surrendering in a street fight.
- Head kicks and stomping are a very real possibility in a street fight.

- Cheap shots, sucker punches, groin strikes, hair pulling, eye gouging, and biting are very common in a real fight. If weapons are present, expect them to be used.
- Expect that the person you are fighting has "friends" that will jump you
- The winner of a fight is usually the one who attacks first and usually by surprise
- Expect more than one person to get involved in a fight that has already started
- Reprieve in a street fight depends on the humanity of the opponent you are facing. If you go down and they don't want to stop, your next stop is the hospital or the morgue
- Going to the ground (and ground fighting) is the last place you want to be in a fight. However, learning how to fight on the ground is essential in this busines
- Women can be as dangerous as men in a fight. Don't underestimate anyone
- If a violent patron can ambush an unsuspecting bouncer, he/she will Alcohol and drugs can build bravado and a false sense of invincibility
- Anger levels will often rise when a person is under the influence of alcohol or drugs
- When you lose control, you get angry, you make mistakes, and this becomes a major weakness in a conflict

THE MYTHOLOGY and REALISM of FIGHTING

The myths regarding street level confrontations are numerous to the extreme. Below are just some common beliefs and misconceptions:

Myth 1: Martial Arts are always effective tools on the street.

Truth: Just like any fighting art, knowing when and where to apply it is the key. While the martial arts (or any fight training) give you skills, too many people try to use them at the wrong time and place. Martial artists are just as susceptible to injuries as anyone else.
Bottom line: No blackbelt will stop a bullet!

Myth 2: Street fighters will always lose to trained fighters.

Truth: Many street fighters are trained fighters. They are trained in specific skills that are quite different than traditional fighters. Street fighters understand the concepts of gross motor skill, overwhelming an opponent, no rule combat, and the 'Dirty Tricks' of fighting. Many people have been defeated by street fighters who have no formal training, just many years of practical experience. Being trained without practical experience (or close simulated experience) is like learning to drive in a video game and then being thrown into a fast car on the street. Hands on experience is a vital part of the learning process.

Myth 3: The kata (trained movements) I have learned will knock an opponent out in 4 moves (or less) guaranteed! My sensei said so.

Truth: While I am not taking away from the importance of martial training (I've been doing it 20 years), nothing, and I do mean NOTHING ever works 100 percent of the time. Like I teach my students, that not all moves work, on all people. Your opponent won't move like your training partners. The violent attacker is going to evade your strikes, hurt you, and take you out.
Don't take what anyone says as TRUTH until you have tested it out yourself!

Myth 4: I've fought several fights in the ring and done very well. I should have no problem against a common street fighter or aggressive patron.

Truth: Victory in one medium (the ring) doesn't mean you should have it in another medium (the street or bar). The reason martial fighters are successful on the street is because their fighting looks nothing like the 'pretty moves in the dojo' or they are able to adapt quickly to the street environment. They realize gross motor skills are king and the complex movements they are taught only work when the opportunity arises. In fact, many martial art moves are performed on the street by martial fighters, but to the untrained eye or observer, it just looks like a "lucky blow or move".

In fact, those are the really interesting fights to watch because if you know what to look for, you can see very successful techniques being used at their basic level with outstanding success.

Myth 5: If I am in a fight and I find myself losing, if I beg or curl up in a ball, my attacker will stop.

Truth: I wouldn't bet on it. Just like women who claim not fighting a rapist is a better solution that fighting them (because they don't want to make the rapist more angry) not fighting when your attacker continues is totally misguided. An attacker is more like to back off if they believe that you are going to continue to fight and cause them damage.

Myth 6: I'll never get taken to the ground in a fight.

Truth: While you are thinking that; your attacker may just dump you on your head. If you don't train for such events and mentally prepare for them, you are surely at a disadvantage. Even the BEST get tackled, trip, fall, or are thrown down.

Myth 7: A grappler will beat a striker.

Truth: This depends on too many factors to make an accurate assessment.
Every fighter believes his martial art system is the best. He has to believe that if he truly wants to master the art. Like the old saying goes: 'It's not the size of the dog in the fight...it's the size of the fight in the dog!'

Myth 8: You can't prepare for a street fight because combat is unpredictable.

Truth: Even water has properties that must conform to certain laws of physics. Just knowing that combat is erratic makes you that much more prepared for the fight. Fighters will do some predictable things depending on the type of martial art they use.

Reality 1: Fights are largely based on gross motor skills not fine motor skills.

The moment knuckles impact your face, unless you are a super-trained combat soldier or fighter (not just a MA practitioner with a black belt) your pain conditioning responses will kick in and nature will takeover. Think about it for a second; human nature, fight or flight, versus ten years of martial arts training. Which do you think your brain is going to pick first? The street fighter understands this (consciously or not) and lets hell fly when the fight begins.

Reality 2: The Fluid nature of combat makes specific patterns of martial arts unusable, at least in the beginning.

Since fighting and combat are fluid (ever changing and flexible), attack A and counter B seldom works as it does in the dojo. The formula usually looks like this: Attack A [street fighter] (with B, C, and D variables thrown in) + Counter from B [martial fighter] (who didn't expect any variables) = Attack A succeeding with overwhelming success! If specific moves are going to be used by trained fighters, you have to wait for the right opening. These 'windows of opportunity' are very seldom there from the get go. By using the fluid nature of combat plus fatigue to your advantage, you may be able to pull off one of those moves. Patience and timing are the essential element of any well placed attack.

Reality 3: You must physically train yourself to prepare for a fight.

This book will show you the door but it is up to you to walk though it. Find a martial art you like, find a good dojo and instructor. Be true to yourself and your art. Practice a lot and train hard. Repetition builds speed and muscle memory. The more you sweat in practice, the less you bleed in combat. Nothing replaces hard work and application of knowledge!

Reality 4: Street fighters while unpredictable, do have traits and physical limitations that you can exploit.

Most street fighters are HEAD HUNTERS, meaning they are trying to hit you in the face and head area with one large hit (slow but strong) or many softer hits (fast but weaker). They use there weaker hand not as a lethal jab but to grab and hold, while punching with the stronger dominate hand.

Most street tough guys smoke and drink excessively thus are not in good shape and get winded easily. This is why most are sucker punchers, needing to end the fight quickly do to lack of stamina.

Bottom line: Never assume or underestimate your opponent. Expect the unexpected.

On the Defensive

Generally, there is nothing wrong with a defensive mindset. Protect yourself with as much force as necessary to prevent or stop the attack. The only problem is that you are constantly measuring yourself against your attacker who gets to pick that level of aggression. You will continue to measure yourself against that scale until he decides to stop or you run out of skill against his attacks. Either way, you are not dictating the pace of the fight. You must choose from the get go to make him fight your fight. As a defensive fighter, that means you must slow down the frequency and strength of his attacks. This is done by throwing off his 'Timing' and fouling up his game plan. For example: when he wants to swing you move, every time he pushes, you pull back. When he rushes forward, you move to the side. Actions such as strikes and counter-strikes, clinches, in and out – side to side movements, these all force him to go defensive and in turn, effectively reverses the roles.

On the Offensive

Offensive fighting for the nightclub security professional is a survival mode.

It is said that a 'good is a great defense'. Thus one does not wait to get struck, then strike back. If an attack is imminent, strike first using the appropriate force needed to stop the threat – PERIOD! The fact is, causing pain and damage is what stops (or ends) the fight.

Bottomline: Being on the offensive means rapid response to a physical attack using the appropriate SAR Matrix level of force.

You must realize that the street fighter is looking for the first strike option (sucker punch) in order to daze or hurt you. The more damage you receive from the start, the less likely you are to put up a good defense. You must also understand that if an attack is launched at you without you being fully ready, you may be caught off guard. Your natural 'flinch response' may take over to cover the area being attacked. From there, you may be able to launch your own counter-attack. I would say that 75% of the time, a sucker punch isn't a sucker punch because the injured party should have seen it coming. This is because he most likely underestimated or ignored the aggressive signs or behavior that should have lead him to set his awareness level on HIGH ALERT. Sucker punches come when you are not facing the attacker or they try and distract you in order to get the first hit. If you just had an encounter, make sure your angles are covered and keep scanning for people in your blind spots. Rarely will someone come up and knock you out when you are standing on the street without probable cause or some sort of warning sign. If that happens, there isn't a thing anyone can do to prevent it. Sucker punches work well because the victim is 'relaxed' and not ready for the blow. There is no resistance to block, absorb or redirect the blow, thus giving the strike a 100% power effectiveness. Always be aware of your surroundings and don't get distracted by others. Fighters will often distract you while their buddy sneaks in from the side for a sucker punch.

The Combative Mindset

Chance favors the prepared mind

When the fight comes your way, the winner of the fight usually is the one who escalates the confrontation the quickest with the most violence at their disposal. You have to be prepared to escalate the intensity of your fight to a point where the other party is either overwhelmed by the attack and submits or is physically unable to continue due to damage caused by you. You must think of a High Low Offensive Attack. That is, strike one place then go to another (head then groin). Keeping your opponent on the defensive allows you to literally beat him though frustration and confusion. Positive thinking and strength of mind will increase your success rate.

Intent: When you attack, have 100% commitment to it.

Improvise: Be prepared to change your tactics at a moments notice. Don't use repetitive moves because they will become easy to counter. Unpredictability is the name of the game!

KYSS: Keep Your System Simple

Your Awareness

The first tool that any person should hone is their awareness. Bouncers/doormen develop a sixth sense over time, which allows them to notice trouble or things out of the ordinary. We are able to identify precursors to violent behavior or people that are in our nightclub/bar for the wrong reasons. Being able to spot trouble before it starts is very important. This is a major part of self-protection. The majority of the time, a person who wants to pick a fight, will send an invitation first. These invitations come in several forms for example:

- They bump into someone for no apparent reason.
- They start an argument for no obvious reason.
- They bow up and begin to act aggressive
- They start using profanities or calling a person out.

Always be aware of your surroundings. Look for people you don't know staring you down or following you around. You are less likely to be attacked if you carry yourself with confidence (not cockiness). Most fighters want to win and are not looking for a fight where they might lose.

Engaging the Attacker

I should point out two distinct forms of conflict: fighting and combat. Some people fight and some people combat one another. What's the difference? Fighting is having a 'winning' mindset, much like when you are in the ring. You inflict just enough damage on your adversary to put him out of commission or make him 'give up' because the fight is too much for him. Combat is the excessive side of a confrontation, not just about winning, it's about SURVIVAL - ending the situation as quickly and fiercely as possible. Making sure your attacker will not come back. Combat uses tricks and tools to injure and even kill an adversary. There are repercussions to combat, that is why so many people engage in fights. If you find yourself in combat, assume that the other person is trying to kill you. **That means you need to protect yourself with DEADLY force if need be, to stop or prevent the life-threatening attack from occurring. This is your legal right!**

Most of the street fighters out there are engaging you on a "fight level". Perhaps to satisfy their ego, their friends, their girlfriends, or their psychopathic tendencies. I know many realists out there cringe at what I am saying. They insist that 'assuming' someone wants to fight instead of combat you is putting yourself in grave danger."

What I am trying to point out here is that MOST people are not trying to kill you, hurt you maybe, injury sometimes, but kill, not really. You have to remember the context in which your potential conflict will occur. This isn't a war zone. If it were, I'd assume that EVERYONE was trying to kill me. On the streets, in front of bars, I assume people want to FIGHT me. See the difference? It doesn't mean you can't change to COMBAT mode if need be, but killing some idiot because he took a swing at you will land you in jail for your excessive force option. Manslaughter or murder, it really doesn't matter because both will ruin your life. So, engaging the attacker with the right attitude is very important. But you've got to engage them with an amount of force they aren't willing to go to. Yes, fights can turn into combat but if you control the pace and dictate how you want to fight, you don't have to go to a combat level.

Will he Attack?

Ask any reality based combat specialist and they'll all say the same thing in regards to violent confrontation. The vast majority of the time, you will be able to read signs, both verbal and non-verbal, that will inform you that an attack is on its way. You just have to train yourself to notice the signs. One such specialist is Darren Laur, who has written 50 articles in regards to combat related subject matter . One such article, 'Street 101', has Mr. Laur explaining the precursors to violent behavior. I have reprinted them here for your study.

Assault Not Imminent But Possible:

- Head, neck, shoulders go back (person making themselves look bigger)
- Face is red, twitching, jerking
- Lips pushed forward bearing teeth (you see the same things in dogs before attack)
- Breathing is fast and shallow (oxygenating the body preparing for fight, flight, hyper vigilance)
- Beads of sweat appear about the face/neck
- Thousand mile glare
- Exaggerated movements
- Finger pointing/ head pecking
- Totally ignores you
- Gives you excessive attention during normal conversation such as direct uninterrupted eye contact
- Goes from totally un-cooperative to totally cooperative (people do not go from hot to cold they de-escalate over time)
- Acts stoned or drunk
- Directs anger towards other inanimate items such as tables, chairs, or walls

If you find yourself confronted by a subject presenting these signs, awareness/self protection strategies should go up, and distance should be created. Your body language should be assertive but not threatening and don't be afraid to allow the person to vent verbally.

Assault Is Imminent:

Face goes from red to white (during a physical confrontation the blood will leave the surface of the body and pool to the big muscles and internal organs of the body needed for survival) In my job as a police officer I see this all the time and when I do one of two things are going to happen, the suspect is either going to fight or run

- Lips tighten over teeth
- Breathing is fast and deep
- Change of stance, their body blades and shoulder drops
- Hands closed into a fist (not uncommon to see the whites of knuckles due to hands being so tight)
- Bobbing up and down or rocking back and forth on feet (this is the bodies way to hide/ mask the initial movement of a first strike)
- Target glace (here you will see your opponent look to where he is going to hit, or where he is going to run/escape)
- Putting head and shin down (body wants to protect the airway, this action does so to a degree)
- Eye brows brought forward into a frown (again the body wants to naturally protect the visual system, this action does so to a degree)

- Stops all movements/ freezes in place
- Dropping center or lowering of body (no different that a cat or dog getting ready to pounce)
- Shedding cloths (very common, you will see your attacker take his hat, coat, shirt, or bag off just prior to the assault)
- One syllable replies (go from full sentences to one syllable replies… reptilian brain is clicking in)

In this group of signs, you have about 1-1.5 seconds to act before your attacker either attacks or runs. If walking and talking your way out is inappropriate or unreasonable, then I teach "First Strike" philosophy, and continue on with a compound attack until your attacker is no longer a risk. In both the Assault not Imminent, and Assault Imminent phases, I do teach my students (in some situations) to bring to the attention of the attacker what they are seeing. Why? The attacker may not know what they are doing. A lot of these signs are autonomic in nature, meaning they happen without conscious thought. The bigger reason, I believe, is for this purpose; most attackers will only attack you when they believe that they have the element of surprise. By sharing with them what you see, you take this primary tactic away from them.

* NOTE: A special Thanks to Darren Laur and Personal Protection Systems for permission to reprint this excerpt.

WHAT IS THE BEST ART TO STUDY FOR BOUNCING?

Many doormen and bouncers skip to this section to see what the self proclaimed professionals have to say about it. We want to offer you suggestions that will keep you and your patrons safe if violence should happen. You have to remember that when we started in this business, the term Mixed Martial Artist hadn't been invented yet. However, I would go out on a limb here and say that good bouncers and doormen have been training in MMA for a long time. You need skills that cover a wide range of situations. Old school bouncers realized that grappling, joint locks, chokes, wrestling, boxing and some weapons work were essential to the job. The professional bouncer cross-trained in a variety of arts to help him deal with the diverse situations that he often encountered in his nightclub/bar.

The following are some martial arts and skill sets that may help you:

Jiu-Jitsu (jujutsu): The traditional Japanese styles that focus on joint locks (wrist locks), throws, take downs, weapon disarms, chokes, and self defense practices. Learning this art for its containment, arresting procedures and come a longs is a must!

Brazilian Jiu-Jitsu: This art can teach you the art and science behind ground fighting, positional dominance, joint locks, submissions, strangles, and body leverage.

Wrestling (Greco or Free Style) or Judo: this art focuses on takedowns, clichés, throws, and ground pinning.

Boxing: Straight up western boxing is unparalleled in teaching someone how to punch, and move on your feet. One of the easiest arts to learn.

Muay Thai: Teaching you the art of the eight limbs (hands, feet, knees and elbows), Muay Thai is a great striking art at long or close range.

What about my style: I've seen bouncers and doormen that have studied ninjutsu and karate that were very good and very well rounded. It all depends on what and how you train. I have also seen doormen that trained in styles that we're primarily "sport" focused or sparring based.

* These styles have no place in a 'no rules environment'.
I know because I am a professional MMA Fighter!

We have to touch upon this because its something that is becoming very prevalent in today's world. With the popularity of the UFC and Mixed Martial Arts competition, there are more people being drawn to the sport. It's exciting, it's popular and many young men today seem to be training in MMA. You would be amazed on how many drunken young guys will tell you that they do "MMA". What they need to remember is "Mixed martial arts are great.. but this ain't the octagon!"

* You must train for the situations that you will encounter as a bouncer/doorman not the octagon.

Arts to Avoid

We are not here to bash on your style or training routine. Some training is better than no training at all. Or is it? Remember, this business requires us to use different techniques under a variety of situations. Use your judgment and do some research. Ask your fellow doormen and bouncers. I've practiced the martial arts for over 20 years and been working the door for twelve. A good martial artist has the ability to change techniques at a moments notice.

*It is this author's professional opinion that a bouncer/doorman should study martial arts that involve a combination of striking and grappling techniques. Find a reputable gym where training is hard, sparing is intense and the overall system is founded on reality based principles of fighting.

How to escort someone out of the bar (passive and active resistance):

As a general rule, Bouncers/Doormen should not touch a patron unless it is absolutely necessary. Asking a patron to leave and giving the person a verbal notification (without touching them) is proper procedure. If the verbal directive doesn't work, you'll need to go the next step. The next step is to gently place your hand on their arm or back with slight pressure in the direction you want them to go. If they walk, great (but be careful, they could turn on you !). If they don't walk you are one step ahead of them. You are able to feel their movement and body positioning. If they tense up or want to strike, your hand will detect the movement. You must move to restrain. The restraint can come in a variety of forms from wristlocks, arm locks, finger locks, or lateral neck restraints. It depends on the situation.

We can't stress this enough. Practice with your team and become skillful at escorting unruly patrons out of the bar. You may be doing it on a regular basis.

*This author strongly advises that when dealing with unruly FEMALE patrons, never escort or remove them without backup. A sexual assault charge could be filed against the bouncer/doorman and the club. <u>Always show up in force and remove the female accordingly</u>.

How to defend against a collar grab: The collar grab happens more than would be expected. Usually a patron will grab onto your collar or front of your shirt when they are trying to resist leaving the bar.

How to defend against a wrist grab: Learn how to pull your hand away properly and use arm bars, wristlocks or take downs when this occurs. Do not just stand there and keep telling the patron to "let go of my wrist please." Once the unruly patron has grabbed you, you have the legal right to defend yourself, using the necessary force needed to stop the threat.

How to defend against a shoulder grab from the rear: This is an important point, because many times people will grab your shoulder when you are trying to restrain someone. Thus having a team member(s) backing you up will usually prevent this from occurring. The saying "Watch my back" is a well-known bouncer term.
* This author recommends if you are alone restraining an unruly patron and someone grabs your shoulder, spin the restrained patron you are holding toward the person who grabbed you. Try to keep the patron you are restraining between you and the other possible threat.
If possible put your back to the wall or a corner until assistance arrives.

How to defend against a choke from behind: Another classic attack on bouncers/doormen is the rear choke. Remember, you must immediately react if this happens. A choke from behind is a sure way in ending up in serious trouble. Force your chin down and turn your head toward the elbow. Drive full force backwards to ram your attacker back against a hard wall or obstacle. If possible, attempt to stomp on the attackers foot or shift sideways and strike the attacker's groin area with a side hand chop.

How to defend against a punch: Movement, distance, and blocking are paramount in defending against punches. Remember, if the attacker is in range, so are you! Put some boxing gloves on with a buddy and practice this drill. It is easier to slip a punch than block one!

How to find a good instructor or school

Finding a good school or instructor is very important to your safety and skill as a nightclub security professional. While many instructors will push their style as the best one, you need to have an objective view of what you are studying. Everything has its strength and weaknesses. That includes martial arts or combat training. Observe a class and talk with some of the students. Do the instructors have good qualifications. Take a look at the facilities. Is it clean? Is it looked after? Most schools offer a 30 day free trial, take advantage of this offer.

Chapter Four:

Building the Machine

To be a good leader one must be a better follower.

For one must know when to lead.. when to follow

and possess the wisdom to know the difference...

Ivan 'Doc' Holiday

'Building the Machine' is this author's own personal terminology, it is defined as "***Having the ability to hire security personnel that have character traits that are compatible in such a way that they can become an elite unit reinforced by each team member's individualistic proficiency***".

When hiring security personnel one must take into account not only the person but also the individual's personality. In this chapter we look at the bouncer who is being hired.

The questions we need to have answered are:

- Does he/she have a criminal record pertaining to violence? Any felony charges?
- Does he/she have mental health issues pertaining to violence? (This is very often over looked. A prime example was the mass murder at Virginia Tech. The assassin had no felonies so he could buy guns, however he had a mental health record that proved him mentally unstable!)
- Does the person have experience in the trade?
- Does he/she have creditable references?
- Does the person interview well?

A good Cooler has only one goal in mind during a face-to-face interview—to obtain the most accurate and positive information possible on each potential bouncer. Coolers don't try to derive "bad" information. They prefer to evaluate bouncers on their positive attributes.

Every interview should have a structure that is clear and transparent to both the interviewers and the potential bouncer.

A simple structure to follow is:

Greeting

Coolers should provide potential bouncers with an outline of the interview process, introduce the participants, tell applicants when they will be able to ask questions and confirm the follow up process.
A gentle introduction puts the candidate at ease. Many potential bouncers will find it difficult to plunge straight into the interview process: it may help to begin by giving some basic information such as the structure of the interview, what the job pertains, etc. This gives the interviewee time to relax. Nerves are not necessarily a reason to mark an interviewee down; beware of prejudging the interviewee at this early stage.

Acquire

Coolers should gather information by use of open, closed and probing questions following agreed question format based on agreed question criteria. Ensure that discriminatory questions are not asked.

Supply

Coolers should supply appropriate and accurate information by being aware of the questions and queries that potential bouncers are likely to ask.

Part

Coolers should ensure that potential bouncers are clear on what happens next, in particular how and when they will hear the outcome of their interview. Ensure that any administrative details that are your responsibility have been dealt with. Ensure that the interviewee is left with an image of professionalism and courtesy - so that regardless of the outcome in their individual case, they will carry away a good impression of the establishment and will feel that they have been dealt with fairly.

It is this author's professional opinion that nightclub and bar owners should not hire security personnel without consulting with or receiving feedback from their head of security/Cooler. It is not to say that the manager or owner does not have the capability to hire good people. The point that is being made is the fact that most security personnel in the head of security position have experience in the field that would be a positive element to the hiring process. Another factor of the hiring process is the assignment of new hired bouncers. If the person hired is experienced and proves him/herself able to function at an acceptable level then all should work well. But if the person is inexperienced or seems a little lost, they should be paired with a more experienced bouncer until they get some experience under their belt. When hiring, the cooler must take into consideration the two vital areas of the nightclub: The Door and the Floor.

Working the door a person must have accomplished doorman experience, for this is a vital area in any establishment.

One does not want a person working the door that has the following problems: Shyness, timid, lethargic or even worse loud-mouthed, rude and forceful. Poor hygiene is a definite no. On the floor the key is teamwork. You do not want to have a person working the floor that is not a team player, prefers to work alone and is withdrawn or has a quick temper and likes to fight.

There are good and bad attributes, especially for the nightclub security professional. According to Jung's theory of Psychological Types we are all different in fundamental ways. One's ability to process different information is limited by their particular type. People can be either Extroverts or Introverts, depending on the direction of their activity; Thinking, Feeling, Sensing, Intuitive, according to their own information pathways; Judging or Perceiving, depending on the method in which they process received information. Now this author does not want to confuse the laymen with a lot of psychological conjecture but it is important to acknowledge the importance of the foundation of an individual's personality.

I will try to explain the following as clearly as possible and keep it in context as it pertains to nightclub security.

Extroverts vs. Introverts

Extroverts are people who are directed towards the objective world whereas Introverts are directed towards the subjective world. The most common differences between Extroverts and Introverts are shown below:

Extroverts

- Are interested in what is happening around them
- Are open and often talkative
- Compare their own opinions with the opinions of others
- Like action and initiative
- Easily make new friends or adapt to a new group
- Say what they think
- Are interested in new people
- Easily break unwanted relations

Introverts

- Are interested in their own thoughts and feelings
- Need to have own territory
- Often appear reserved, quiet and thoughtful
- Usually do not have many friends
- Have difficulties in making new contacts
- Like concentration and quiet
- Do not like unexpected visits and therefore do not make them
- Work well alone

Overall, you can't really change your basic personality, nor do you need to in some cases. A particular personality trait is two-sided—useful in some situations, not so helpful in others. For example this author has had ADHD (Attention Deficit Hyperactivity Disorder) since childhood. Adults with ADHD often have a difficult time with that first impression. Their hyperactivity and inattentiveness is sometimes misinterpreted as a lack of respect or interest. But there is a plus side to this, many ADHD adults have the ability to multi-task, problem solve and think outside the box. By analyzing how your innate traits affect your health, well-being and ability to function you can come up with strategies to channel your traits in a positive way. Thus such traits are very important when 'Building the machine'. Overall, one does not want to hire an introvert personality to work as a bouncer given their individualistic way of thinking. What a cooler is looking for in his bouncers/doormen when hiring is based on the following points:

- The person should be in good physical condition.
- The person should have good temperament.
- The person should have good hygiene and professional appearance.
- The person should be able to read, write and speak well.
- The person should have a team player attitude.
- The person should have a positive personality.
- The person should like to work with people and enjoy social gatherings.
- The person should dislike fighting and physical aggression.
- The person should have no felony record or history of violence.

Background Checks

This author has advocated this particular issue for the past 20 years. It is common sense that one does not hire a bouncer/doorman who has felony charges pertained to violence of any kind. However, if a person had a juvenile criminal record in the past but over the years had matured and has become a law-abiding adult, this person should be considered for employment. Again this is at the discretion of the employer. Many security companies will do background checks for $35-$50 dollars per person. This is a small price to pay when one considers the cost of a lawsuit.

REMEMBER -When hiring, the employer is held legally responsible and accountable for the illegal behavior of their employees.

This author knows many, very good doormen/bouncers, who have juvenile criminal records. Many believe that when they become a legal adult their juvenile criminal records are erased. This is not true! Although many people think that juvenile records are destroyed after a person becomes an adult; juvenile records are not automatically "sealed" or "expunged" when a juvenile reaches the age of legal adulthood.

The laws vary from state to state/province to province but in general to have records expunged a petition with this request should be filed with the court. This is a legal matter and it is recommended that an attorney be consulted if you wish to pursue this. Be careful with this topic! A crime can be erased from your file's history [or taken off of your 'record'], but a specific act you have taken cannot be erased from your own history. Once you commit an ACT [example- a crime], you can never erase that ACT from your past.

What does it mean to "seal" a juvenile record?

A record only can be "sealed" three years after a person has finished serving his or her sentence for a crime. Sealing removes the record from the main record file and secures it in a separate file available only to a restricted group of readers. Judges in later criminal cases against the same person can still use sealed juvenile records, even after the person becomes an adult. If the police or a court asks about the record of a person whose record has been sealed, they are told that the person has a "sealed delinquency record over 3 years old." All other people that ask about the record are told that the person has "no record."

What does it mean to "expunge" a record?

Expunging a record destroys the record entirely. Juvenile records cannot be expunged in some states, although several other states do allow some form of expunging. A few states do not allow courts to seal or expunge records at all.

How can I seal a juvenile record?

A person with a juvenile record must wait three years after completely serving his or her sentence for the crime before applying to seal the record. In addition, the person cannot have been found guilty of any crime, except for minor traffic offenses, anywhere in the United States within the three years before making the application.

Overall it is a good idea to have your juvenile criminal record expunged. This will make getting employment especially in the security field more obtainable.

Chapter Five:

-Conflict Resolution-

The Psychology of Bouncing

Hence to fight and conquer in all your battles
is not supreme excellence; supreme excellence consists
in breaking the enemy's resistance without fighting.

SunTzu – Art of War

Patron Personality

The human mind is truly a mysterious entity. As Albert Einstein put it:

The most beautiful experience we can have is the mysterious. It is the fundamental emotion that stands at the cradle of true art and true science...

Psychology is the scientific study of human behavior. As both an academic and applied discipline, Psychology involves the scientific study of mental processes such as perception, cognition, emotion, personality, as well as environmental influences, such as social and cultural influences, and interpersonal relationships, in order to devise theories of human behavior. Psychology also refers to the application of such knowledge to various spheres of human activity including problems of individuals' daily lives and the treatment of mental health problems. Social psychology is the study of how social conditions affect human beings. What does this have to do with nightclub security? A Bouncer/Doorman must have the ability to identify the stages of aggressive behavior and understand the mindset of their unruly patrons. Thus it is important to understand what anger and aggressive behavior entails. Anger is a completely normal, usually healthy, human emotion. But when it gets out of control and turns destructive, it can lead to problems—problems at work, in your personal relationships, and in the overall quality of your life. And it can make you feel as though you're at the mercy of an unpredictable and powerful emotion. Not only does the bouncer/doorman have to deal with the anger of the aggressive patron but he/she must control his or her own anger.

Anger is "*an emotional state that varies in intensity from mild irritation to intense fury and rage*," according to Charles Spielberger, PhD, a psychologist who specializes in the study of anger. Like other emotions, it is accompanied by physiological and biological changes; when you get angry, your heart rate and blood pressure go up, as do the levels of your energy hormones, adrenaline, and non-adrenaline. Anger can be caused by both external and internal events. A patron could be angry with a specific person (such as a drinking buddy or girlfriend) or event (loss of a job, death of a friend..etc) or their anger could be caused by worrying or brooding over personal problems.

Memories of traumatic or enraging events can also trigger anger and aggressive behavior. The instinctive, natural way to express anger is to respond aggressively. Anger is a natural, adaptive response to threats; it inspires powerful, often aggressive feelings and behaviors, which allow us to fight and defend ourselves when we are attacked. A certain amount of anger, therefore, is necessary to our survival. On the other hand, we can't physically lash out at every person or object that irritates or annoys us; laws, social norms, and common sense place limits on how far our anger can take us. Anger can be suppressed, and then converted or redirected. This happens when you hold in your anger, stop thinking about it, and focus on something positive. The aim is to inhibit or suppress your anger and convert it into more constructive behavior. The danger in this type of response is that if it isn't allowed outward expression, your anger can turn inward—on yourself.

Anger turned inward may cause hypertension, high blood pressure, or depression. Unexpressed anger can create other problems. It can lead to pathological expressions of anger, such as passive-aggressive behavior (getting back at people indirectly, without telling them why, rather than confronting them head-on) or a personality that seems perpetually cynical and hostile. This type of patron can be a serious problem. A patron who refuses to let go of the situation and could come back later to start trouble again. People who are constantly putting others down, criticizing everything, and making cynical comments haven't learned how to constructively express their anger. According to Jerry Deffenbacher, PhD, a psychologist who specializes in anger management, some people really are more "hotheaded" than others are; they get angry more easily and more intensely than the average person does. There are also those who don't show their anger in loud spectacular ways but are chronically irritable and grumpy. Easily angered people don't always curse and fight; sometimes they withdraw socially, sulk, or get physically ill. People who are easily angered generally have what some psychologists call a low tolerance for frustration, meaning simply that they feel that they should not have to be subjected to frustration, inconvenience, or annoyance.

They can't take things in stride, and they're particularly infuriated if the situation seems somehow unjust: for example, being corrected for a minor mistake or a patron asked to leave the establishment.

What makes these people this way? A number of things. One cause may be genetic or physiological: There is evidence that some children are born irritable, touchy, and easily angered, and that these signs are present from a very early age. Another may be sociocultural. Anger is often regarded as negative; we're taught that it's all right to express anxiety, depression, or other emotions but not to express anger. As a result, we don't learn how to handle it or channel it constructively. Research has also found that family background plays a role. Typically, people who are easily angered come from families that are abusive, disruptive, chaotic, and not skilled at interpersonal communications.

De-escalation Techniques of the SAR Matrix

When dealing with unruly patrons we must follow ethical and professional guidelines. The following is a brief synopsis of what we need to do to attain a win-win situation when confronted with an unruly patron.

- Look at conflict in its entirety and maintain the conflict at a verbal level.
- Remain professional and under control during disagreements.
- Find solutions to produce a Win-Win outcome.
- Maintain professionalism in any context.
- Be careful not to become over-bearing and violate personal space.
- Avoid using language that expresses personal feelings during conflicts.
- Employ empathy to connect with people while maintaining professionalism.
- Use words that are on-target by first understanding the patron's point of view.
- Ensure that the patron comprehends your words and actions.
- Achieve cooperation and break through uncertainty, confusion, anger, mistrust and prejudice.
- Communicate without shaming, blaming or manipulating.

* If the unruly patron takes the situation to a physical level follow the SAR Matrix guidelines and respond with appropriate force.

Managing Aggression

A Definition of Violence:

'Any incident in which a person is abused, threatened, or assaulted. This includes an explicit or implicit challenge to their safety, well-being or health. The resulting harm may be physical, emotional or psychological.'

The effective handling of aggressive patrons is one of the most demanding aspects of working in an establishment. It is an area where good interaction and communication skills are required. The majority of situations, where there is a potential for violence, can be handled using the three most important factors in bouncing :

Teamwork, Communication, and Position.

A Definition of Aggression:

'Any behavior that is perceived by the victim as being deliberately harmful and damaging either psychologically or physically'.

* The overall goal is to prevent the aggression from escalating into actual physical violence.

Signs of aggression:

- Standing tall (bowing up)
- Red faced
- Raised voice
- Rapid breathing

- Direct prolonged eye contact
- Exaggerated gestures

Patrons may become aggressive for a number of reasons, including:

- Intoxication
- Frustration
- Unfairness
- Humiliation
- Immaturity
- Excitement
- Learned Behavior (Behavior that got results in the past)
- Reputation
- Means to an end
- Decoy

The following signs may indicate aggression:

- Any major change in behavior that is not normal for a particular patron
- Pale or flushed face
- Rising voice, cussing
- Focusing/narrowing of the gaze
- Tensing of muscles
- Clenched fists
- Increased agitation and disturbance in behavior (example: ranting, pacing, throwing or hitting things like walls and chairs ..etc)

Security faced with aggressive patrons should assess the risk of violence by considering the following:

- Is the patron facing a high level of stress?
  - (Example: a recent bereavement, loss of employment, divorce)
- Does the patron seem to be drunk or on drugs?
- Does the patron have a history of violence?
- Does the patron have a history of psychiatric illness?
- Has the patron verbally abused security in the past?
- Has the patron threatened security with violence in the past?

Communication

Communication is a two-way process that relates to verbal interaction (listening, speaking and hearing), non-verbal interaction (interpretation and observational skills - looking and seeing).

To minimize communication problems security should use language appropriate to the patron (in his/her language if possible and using an interpreter where necessary), take time to communicate, encourage and give feedback, and make sure the conversation takes place at an appropriate time and place (where possible).

Some of the common inhibitions to effective communication are:

- Noise
- Language
- Perception and prejudice
- Intrusion of personal space

We cannot necessarily avoid or overcome all these barriers but we need to find ways of minimizing them.

Noise:

Noise is a major distraction when trying to communicate. It's hard to hold a discussion against a noisy background.

Language:

Security needs to converse in a direct and explicit manner. Avoid emotive language. (For example – avoid 'power' words and cussing)

Perception and Prejudice:

Everybody has a unique background and history with influences and experiences that form our way of looking at the world. It is important to recognize our prejudices for what they are and to work round the prejudices of others. We have to maintain a professional attitude by not allowing our own perceptions to get in the way of our duties and responsibilities towards others or to let our prejudices influence the way we communicate.

Intrusion of personal space:

Avoid standing too close to the person. Patrons who are stressed tend to feel 'trapped' or 'controlled' when their personal space is violated. Allow a comfortable but guarded distance between yourself and the patron. The distance is gauged by patron posture/ body language versus your own personal safety and ability to handle the situation.

Non-verbal Communication

Security should be aware of non-verbal messages that demonstrate how a patron is feeling or may respond. Security should apply the techniques of non-verbal communication they are taught in training to help defuse potentially violent situations.

De-fusion Strategies

Before anything else happens security should seek to defuse the situation. A patron who is out of control will be under the influence of an 'Adrenaline Rush'. Security should aim to do nothing to escalate their state of mind while being prepared to defend themselves if necessary.

Security should seek to:

- Appear confident
- Displaying calmness
- Create some space
- Speak slowly, gently and clearly
- Lower your voice
- Avoid staring
- Avoid arguing and confrontation
- Show that they are listening
- Calm the patron before trying to solve the problem

Security should adopt a non-threatening body posture:

- Use a calm, open posture (sitting or standing)
- Reduce direct eye contact (as it may be taken as a confrontation)
- Allow the patron adequate personal space
- Keep both hands visible
- Avoid sudden movements that may startle or be perceived as an attack
- Avoid audiences – as an audience may escalate the situation

*NEVER THREATEN

Once you have made a threat or given an ultimatum you have ceased all negotiations and forced yourself into a potential win-lose situation.

- Explain your purpose or intention
- Give clear, brief, assertive instruction, negotiate options and avoid threats.
- Whenever possible -Move towards a 'safe zone'.
  - (Example: avoid being trapped in a corner, some place with less noise away from the crowd and loud music).
- Encourage an explanation (for their behavior)
- Encourage reasoning by the use of open questions and enquire about the reason for the aggression.
- Questions about the 'facts' rather than the feelings can assist in de-escalating (Example: what has caused you to feel angry?)
- Show genuine positive regard through non-verbal and verbal responses.
- Listen carefully and show empathy, acknowledge any grievances, concerns or frustrations. Don't patronize their concerns.
- Ensure that your non-verbal communication is non-threatening
- Consider which de-escalation techniques are appropriate for the situation.
- Pay attention to non-verbal clues (Example: eye contact and body movement). Allow more personal space than normal.
- Be aware of your own non-verbal behavior, such as body posture and eye contact.
- Appear calm, self controlled and confident without being unsympathetic or overassertive.

(SAR) Security Action Response Matrix.

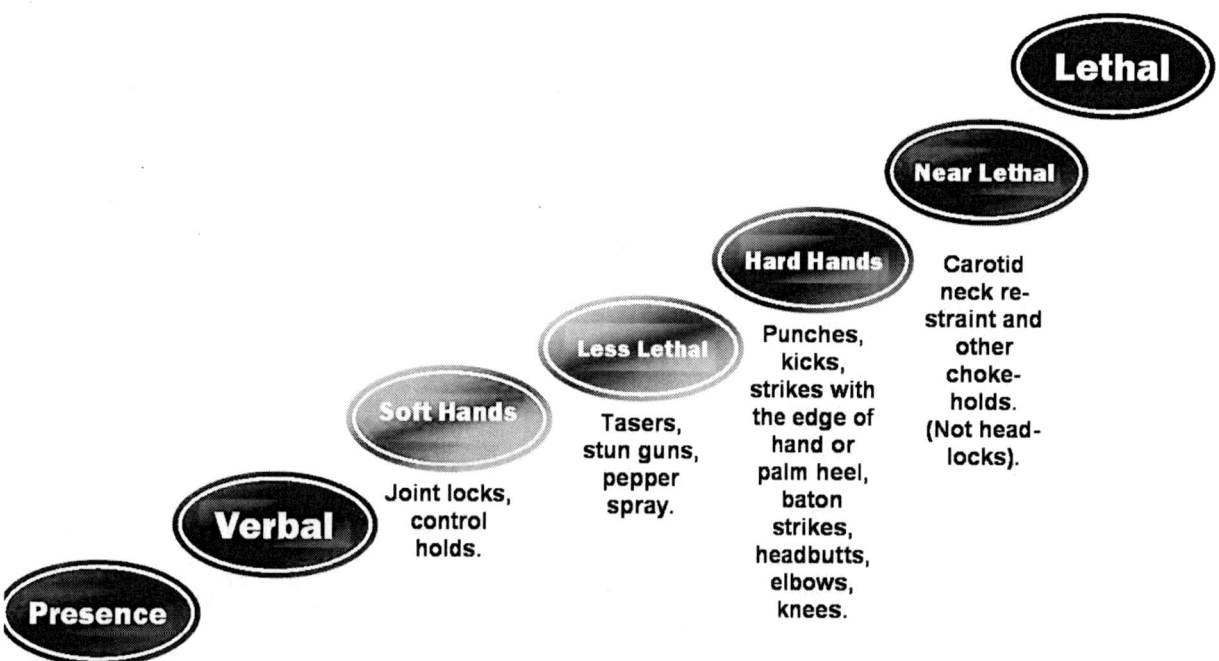

This is basically a modified version of the force continuum has been around for years and is still taught at most police academies. The force continuum is broken down into six broad levels. Each level is designed to have a degree factor as the need for force changes as the situation dictates. It is common for the level of force to go from level two, to level three, and back again in a matter of seconds.

Level One

Security Personnel Presence: The mere presence of a highly visible Bouncer/Doorman or a number of security personnel is often enough to stop unruly behavior. Without saying a word, an alert Bouncer/Doorman can deter unruly patrons by use of body language and gestures. At this level gestures should be non-threatening and professional.

Level Two

Verbal Intervention: Used in combination with a visible presence, the use of the voice can usually achieve the desired results. Words can be whispered, used normally, or shouted to be effective. The content of the message is as important as your demeanor. It's always best to start out calm but firm and non-threatening. A low voice forces the person to listen. Choice of words and intensity can be increased as necessary or used in short commands in serious situations. The right combination of words in combination with Bouncer/Doorman presence can de-escalate a tense situation and prevent the need for a physical altercation. Training and experience improves the ability of a Bouncer/Doorman to communicate effectively with everyone including the police.

Level Three

<u>Physical Intervention (soft hands)</u>: Certain situations may arise where words alone do not reduce the aggression. Sometimes security personnel will need to get involved physically. At this level, minimal force would involve the use of bare hands to guide, hold, and restrain. This does not include offensive moves such as punching, tackling, and choking. Pain compliance holds could apply here, but only after ordinary holds fail to control an aggressive patron. The overall goal here is 'Containment' for the protection of other patrons, security and the violent patron being restrained. A Tactical Baton can only be used at this level as a self-defense mechanism to block blows or temporarily restrain a violent patron only.

<u>* A Tactical Baton can be used ONLY if the doorman has been properly trained and certified to do so with permission from the establishment and local Law Enforcement. It should only be used on a person who exhibits physical violence.</u>

Chemical Agent's: Sometimes when the violent patron is physically aggressive or violent, more extreme, but non-deadly measures must be used in defense to bring the violent patron under control. Before moving to level four, it is assumed that other less physical measures had been tried or was deemed inappropriate. When used by surprise, OC pepper spray is an excellent distraction, allowing the Bouncer/Doorman time to get away, call the police, or subdue a violent patron.

* OC Pepper Spray can be used ONLY if the doorman has been properly trained and certified to do so with permission from the establishment and local Law Enforcement.

Contrary to media advertising, pepper spray does not have stopping power or cause paralysis. An assailant can still grab you, punch you, stab you, or shoot you and will definitely be angrier after being sprayed. Also, OC Pepper spray may not always be effective on the insane, addicts, intoxicated, or hysterical persons.

* It is this author's professional opinion that OC Pepper Spray should NEVER be used inside an establishment in self-defense, to protect property or to enforce club rules.

Pepper Spray needs to be used in a controlled environment.
Remember it's a defensive weapon. Pepper spray needs to be directed in the violent patron's face for maximum result and not sprayed wildly at groups of people. Even though considered non-deadly, chemical sprays can cause severe reaction and even death to a violent patron with medical or allergic conditions. Also, pepper sprays have a blinding effect and care must be used that spray victims do not fall down stairs or walk in front of oncoming traffic.

Remember: When forced to use OC pepper spray on a violent patron at a level 4 threat, you are responsible for the personal safety of the person.
"Support – Offer First-Aid – Call the Police".

Level Four

Non-Lethal Weapons: To use force under level four means that the situation was so extreme, violent, and immediate that it was necessary to temporarily incapacitate a violent patron prior to arrival of the police. This includes the use of all methods of non-deadly force beginning with the empty hand up through and including impact tools. At level four, properly used defensive and offensive techniques are allowed under the right circumstances. Choke holds and carotid neck holds can be used, but at great risk. Although still taught at many self-defense academies, neck compressions are very risky and used only in extreme situations. **Tactical Baton blows to the violent patron's head or throat can be deadly and are <u>inconsistent with professional training standards at this level</u>.** Temporary incapacitation is used to stop a violent patron from injuring you or others long enough to restrain them. Tactical Baton blows to Green or Yellow MEB Chart Zones (soft tissue and certain joint areas) are all consistent with professional security training standards at this level.

Level Five

Deadly Force: When you are in immediate fear of death or great bodily injury at the hands of a violent patron you are authorized to use deadly force in most states. Your hands, impact tools, etc can apply deadly force. There are no rules, other than negligence, for applying deadly force when it is justified. However, deadly force is the highest standard and must be justified. This SAR Matrix will be considered in the aftermath as an assessment to see if other alternatives were used first or would of been more appropriate.

*For nightclub security personnel a firearm should not be on your person or in the club at anytime.

To fully understand the SAR –Security Action Response Matrix it must be periodically discussed and reviewed by all security personnel. Practical rehearsal of exercises will help reinforce the training and cause the reactions to become more natural, accurate and conscientious instead of instinctive. In a crisis situation, fear and adrenalin have a way of accelerating the SAR Matrix. Practice and ongoing training exercises will also ease the effects of stress by implementing confidence and self-control.

Situational Force

Matching a bouncer/doorman's response to a situation should be a strong consideration when force options are initiated. However, a bouncer/doorman's response can be influenced by other factors. For example, a 6' 5" tall, 315 lbs professional wrestler charges a bouncer/doorman as he/she is attempting to stop him for beating and injuring a bartender. The bouncer/doorman is 5' 6" tall and weighs 165 lbs. It is clear that there is a disparity in height and weight between the aggressive patron and the bouncer/doorman, which tips the scale toward the aggressive patron. The scale may be tipped even further due to the violent patron's familiarity with hand-to-hand skills as a professional wrestler. Gender may also be a factor. When these specific differences are taken into consideration, the security personnel, in this example, may indeed need to use a higher response level than generally indicated by the SAR Matrix. Other factors that could also influence the use of a higher force option by security personnel that may include, but are not limited to, the following: age, fatigue, involvement of multiple attackers, a security personnel/violent patron's physical impairment (i.e. rheumatoid arthritis, prosthetics, etc.), or a violent patron's impairment caused by a mental health and/or substance abuse problem.

The Police

When dealing with the police, fire marshal, or liquor control inspector, always cooperate fully and in a professional manner. You are a representative of the club and if you treat them in a negative manner, you and your establishment will live to regret such a foolish error! We are on the same side; the side of what is right and just.

No one can shut a club down faster than the Fire Marshal! He is looking for fire safety code violations and especially the legal Seating Capacity of your establishment. You will find this on the business license that should be posted in plain site. Add to this the fact that you can't support a nightclub or bar without a liquor license. Remember, respect goes a long way in this business. The police are a bouncer's heavy artillery. Always attempt to have a good rapport with the local police department. Get to know a few of the police officers by name. I don't encourage you to call the police for every little infraction that occurs. Only call the police if a crime has occurred, someone has been seriously injured and requires an ambulance, or there are so many people fighting that it is impossible to stop it with your entire door staff. Many nightclub/bar owners don't like it when the police get involved in situations regarding the club. Thus is the Catch 22 - It brings negative publicity to the nightclub not only in the eye's of the public, but the Alcohol Beverage Commission and the insurance companies as well. This can cause trouble for the establishment later on, when it is time to renew their liquor license, liability insurance or a property lease.

Report Writing: It's All In The Paperwork

This author recommends that : <u>Every establishment should have a SECURITY LOGBOOK to keep a daily record of all security activity and reports. This needs to be kept up to date by the head of security and read before the start of every shift.</u>

There is a saying in private security, law enforcement, and the judicial system that sums up the importance of report writing:

<u>"If it's not on paper, it didn't happen."</u>

Most security and law enforcement personnel despise paperwork. Most top sales people hate it too. Sales people can pass it on to the secretary as long as they are a top producer. We have to do it ourselves, no matter how productive we are. We may be the complainant, witness, or the person to whom the incident was reported. As such, we have to be the one to write down what we saw, heard , smelled, tasted, or felt. This written account will become an important part of any subsequent civil or criminal proceedings. This orginal report can not be amended changed or corrected, once it is written.

Supplemental reports can be added later to clarify points or add information, but the original report is the most important.

The Importance of Complete and Accurate Reports

If an attorney questions you at a deposition or actual trial, he will ask you about an incident you were somehow involved in. He or she may want you to recall what someone did or didn't do during a particular incident.

He or she may ask you about anything that occurred before, during or afterwards. You may feel that you have a good memory and that you will be able to answer with clear recollection, but attorneys will question your memory. Cases take a long time to get to the first stage of action, and anyone can forget important details. Most of us will need an accurate report to refresh our memories, in order to testify professionally. Courts and juries want the corroboration of a report that was written soon after the incident. If it's not in your report, the opposing attorney will ask you why? He will imply that if you didn't write it down, you are recalling something after the fact in order to bolster your case. **Save yourself some trouble and embarrassment, write complete and accurate reports** . Even though you may despise paperwork and may not write like an author, you can still compile a good report. Manage to get the facts down in logical order, completely yet concisely, and you will have written a good report. Judges, juries, your company's attorney, and your supervisor will realize that you are a night club bouncer not an English professor.

The Contents of the Report

You probably heard of the five W's and H. Your report should answer these six questions:

- o Who?
- o What?
- o When?
- o Where?
- o Why?
- o How?

Some of the questions might have more than one answer.

<u>WHO</u>

- o Who was involved in the incident
- o Who were the police officers who responded?
- o Who were the suspects?
- o Who was injured?
- o Who were the witnesses?
- o Who reported this to you ?
- o Who found the evidence?
- o Who started it?
- o Who called the police?

WHAT

- o What happened?
- o What did each involved person do?
- o What weapons were used?
- o What was said by those involved?
- o What was damaged or stolen ?
- o What did you do?
- o What did the witness see?
- o What is the police incident report number?
- o What did the police do ?
- o What injuries were sustained ?

When

- o When did the incident occur?
- o When did it start?
- o When did it end?
- o When did you get there?
- o When did the police arrive?
- o When was the problem discovered?
- o When was it reported?

Where

- o Where did the incident occur?
- o Where were the witnesses?
- o Where were you?
- o Where were the missing items last seen?
- o Where were they found?
- o Where were the suspects?
- o Where were the injured parties taken?
- o Where did the involved parties live?

Why

- o Why did the perpetrator act?
- o Why did the others act?
- o Why did you act?
- o Why wasn't the perpetrator stopped sooner?
- o Why did you do what you did?
- o Why did you call the police?
- o Why did the police do whatever they did?
- o When did you get there?

HOW

- o How did the person get hurt?
- o How was the injured person transported?
- o How did the person get in ?
- o How did the person get out?
- o How did the person know where the valuables were ?
- o How did the perpetrator bypass the alarm system?

Incident Report Forms

Police departments and security agencies have their own incident report forms. These incident reports eliminate much of the narrative with a simple fill-in-the-blank format. **Be sure to log the report number and info in your Security Log Book. Keep the hardcopy report on file.**

What's In It For You?

On a personal note, good reports are essential, because your reports may be one of the only ways your boss has of evaluating your performance. He may not be there when the incidents happen, but when he reads your concise, complete reports, your professional performance will be known to him. Write hurried, incomplete, and disorganized reports, and you will appear to be unprofessional, and not as competent as you are. On the other hand, someone who is not as proficient at their job, but writes good reports, will appear to have performed much better than he actually did.

Security Incident Report   File #_____

Type of Incident _____ Location: _____Date/Time: _____

Person#1: _____ DOB: _____ Sex: _____

Address:

_____

Phone: _____

Person#2: _____ DOB: _____ Sex: _____

Address:

_____

Phone: _____

If more people involved, use another form and just fill in their info, leave rest blank.

What Happened?

Describe Injuries and how received:

_____

_____

_____

_____

_____

_____

_____

_____

_____

_____

_____

_____

Property Involved? Whose? Describe Property and Damage. Approx Loss: $ _____

_____

_____

_____

Witness & Suspect Information: _____

_____

_____

_____

_____

_____

_____

_____

_____

_____

_____

Ambulance/Hospital: _____

Police involved? Officer: _____**Agency:** _____ **#**_____ **Report #** _____

Disposition of Evidence:

_____

Security Name: _____ **Signature:** _____ **Date:** _____

Chapter Six:

Working the Door

"I have no data yet. It is a capital mistake to theorize before one has data. Insensibly one begins to twist facts to suit theories, instead of theories to suit facts."

-Sherlock Holmes, in "A Scandal in Bohemia"

Why does this author refer to working the door as the true art of bouncing? There is so much more to working as a bouncer/doorman then just physically removing unruly patrons. The true art of the professional doorman is having the ability to see what other's do not. To study the patrons coming into the club and determine if they are potential trouble. To further explore this art we must first look at the true master of perception – Sherlock Holmes. Though just a fictional character from the intellectual writings of the great literary author Sir Conan Arthur Doyle. Sherlock Holmes is a hero, in that he solves cases and repeatedly saves London from the forces of evil. It is his strong power of perception that solves the crimes, and it is his hunger for intellectual challenge and perfection that drives his crime solving skills. To succeed as a detective Holmes frequently must himself descend into London's underworld. To the professional Bouncer/Doorman the Power of Perception is his greatest tool. It can be honed razor sharp by possessing an inquisitive mind and exceptional eye for detail. Perception is the process of acquiring, interpreting, selecting, and organizing sensory information. The word perception comes from the Latin perception-, percepio, meaning "receiving, collecting, action of taking possession, apprehension with the mind or senses."

Take for example these two Ambiguous images.
What do you see? A 3-D box and a Vase? Or do you see a box at different angles? Or perhaps the vase is not a vase but two people facing each other.

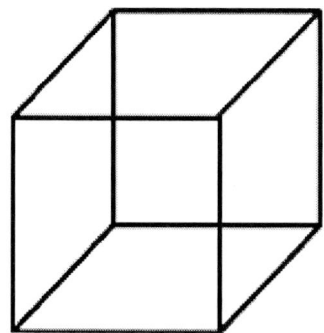 

Thus the power of perception has been a true advantage to this author over the years. Examining a person entails: their body language, eye contact, listening to the tone of their voice, smelling liquor on their breath, seeing needle marks on their arm, observing gang related clothing (colors or patches), distinguishing the shape of a gun in their pocket, or a weapon in their boot. From the information you gather you create in your mind an image of the person and formulate a plan of action. Bouncer/Doormen are very similar to professional poker players in the aspect of reading their opposition. Although they are generally not aware of it, many people send and receive non-verbal signals all the time. These signals may indicate what they are truly feeling.

The technique of 'reading' people is used frequently. For example, the idea of mirroring body language to put people at ease is commonly used in interviews. It sets the person being interviewed at ease. Mirroring the body language of someone else indicates that they are understood. One of the most basic and powerful body-language signals is when a person crosses his or her arms across the chest. This can indicate that a person is putting up an unconscious barrier between themselves and others. It can also indicate that the person is cold. When the overall situation is amicable, it can mean that a person is thinking deeply about what is being discussed. But in a serious or confrontational situation, it can mean that a person is expressing opposition. This is especially so if the person is leaning away from the speaker. A harsh or blank facial expression often indicates outright hostility. Such a person is not an ally, and may be considering contentious tactics. Consistent eye contact can indicate that a person is thinking positively of what the speaker is saying. Individuals with anxiety disorders are often unable to make eye contact without discomfort. It can also mean that the other person doesn't trust the speaker enough to "take his eyes off" the speaker. Lack of eye contact can indicate negativity. Eye contact is often a secondary and misleading gesture because we are taught from an early age to make eye contact when speaking. If a person is looking at you but is making the arms-across-chest signal, the eye contact could be indicative that something is bothering the person, and that he wants to talk about it. Or if while making direct eye contact a person is fiddling with something, even while directly looking at you, it could indicate the attention is elsewhere.

Disbelief is often indicated by averted gaze, or by touching the ear or scratching the chin. So is eyestrain, or itchiness. When a person is not being convinced by what someone is saying, the attention invariably wanders, and the eyes will stare away for an extended period. Boredom is indicated by the head tilting to one side, or by the eyes looking straight at the speaker but becoming slightly unfocused. A head tilt may also indicate a sore neck, and unfocused eyes may indicate vision or eye problems in the listener. It should be noted that some people (Example: people with certain disabilities, or those on the autistic spectrum) use and understand body language differently, or not at all. Interpreting their gestures and facial expressions (or lack thereof) in the context of normal body language usually leads to misunderstandings and misinterpretations (especially if body language is given priority over spoken language). It should also be stated that people from different cultures interpret body language in different ways. In our daily lives we encounter many forms of body language, these are a few examples:

Stress - shaking of legs; wetting one's lips frequently
Lying -touching the face; or putting a hand over the mouth
   o Pulling at the ears; scratching the nose
   o Casting eyes down, or looking downward to the left
   o Shifting in the seat
   o Also wiping hands on trousers to get rid of sweat or fidgeting with hands.

Rejection - crossed or folded arms, leaning back

Defiance - frowning; hands on hips

Aggression - leaning far forward or clenched fists; squaring of shoulders, stiffening of posture, tensing of muscles

Anxiety - Massaging temples, different than normal breathing rates, hunched shoulders, nervous head movements

The Nightclub security professional needs to sharpen his people reading skills to aid him/her in detecting troublemakers and removing them before they cause trouble. This is especially critical when dealing with potentially dangerous patrons such as psychopaths and violent criminal types.

Checking Age Identification

Every nightclub differs on what they allow for identification and entry into their establishment. A Government issued photo ID is the only thing that you should accept - PERIOD! The laws regarding this are very clear and you are taking a huge risk if you allow someone to use a Student Card, Bus Pass, or just a Birth Certificate to get in. Once a club is known for letting in under age patrons, the police won't be far behind. The police will send under age patrons to your club to test your security. They will try and see if the doormen can be bribed or if he is paying attention while on duty. With the advancement of computers and laser printers, fake driver's licenses are becoming easier to produce and even easier to buy off the Internet.

Most modern IDs are produced in hard plastic rather than the older lamination style. These IDs have several security features such as holograms, microprint, 2D bar codes and magnetic strip information. Today new encoded holograms are imbedded in the state and provincial ID's that can only be revealed under UV light. **This author recommends that bouncers carry UV/LED flashlights to check ID's.** Young people often use older style lamination IDs, and usually from a state or country that they assume you have never seen before. **There are books out there that list all the driver's licenses of North America.** In some cases, young people will alter one number on the license to make them of age. If you have a keen eye, you should be able to catch these fakes with no problem. In the majority of cases minors use an older persons ID who has the similar facial features. Most ABC or ABT state offices will send out an officer to teach your security ID techniques FREE OF CHARGE! This author advises nightclub and bar security to take advantage of this. It is not only advantageous but it shows the state liquor control board that your establishment is making a serious attempt to enforce the state liquor laws.

A nightclub/bar should accept only four types of ID:

> **Passport**
> **Provincial or State Drivers License**
> **Provincial or State ID card**
> **Military ID**

These items should be at the door at all times:

- ✓ UV light to check ID's and Cover charge money
- ✓ A flashlight and security radio.
- ✓ Cell phone or club phone. (With speed dial for 911 or police)
- ✓ ID stamp or wristbands. (UV Stamps are popular today)
- ✓ A sign, which clearly states the Rule & Regulations of the club.
- ✓ A list of birth signs taped somewhere for reference.
- ✓ If possible, invest in an ID scanner.
- ✓ Have a pen and paper for signature checks and field notes.
- ✓ Security Log Book that records all nightclub issues that deal with security. The cooler can keep a record of all previous events.

When a patron comes up to you, you should have a system where there is a rope between you and them. In fact, there should be a roped area all around you and the front door. It should remain empty most of the time, only allowing people to pass through the door and into the establishment when you have checked their ID's. Patrons should not be leaving the same way they came in. There should be some sort of separated 'Enter' and 'Exit'. It is also important to watch the exiting patron's. A patron should not leave your club with alcohol drinks or stolen property. While standing at the divided door area, you greet the customers with the traditional, "Welcome to the club. IDs please." Always bring the patron within the range of the security camera. The camera protects you and the nightclub in case of any unexpected events that might happen. If your club doesn't have video surveillance, I suggestion you speak to the owners about installing a security camera system. In this author's professional opinion a good security camera system is priceless!

Being a vigilant doorman, you should - if you are not busy - be looking out past your spot at the door and notice the people coming and going. Be on a look out for overly intoxicated people and groups of young people standing close together outside your door. This is usually the time where they are talking about how to get into your nightclub (when they are underage).

What are age identification policies and how do they work?

Age identification policies are written guidelines that provide employees instructions on checking age identification of customers that enter a nightclub or bar and attempt to buy alcohol.

These guidelines will help keep under aged patrons out of your club:

- Encouraging your bartenders to refuse to sell alcohol to any customer who does not have a valid state ID showing he/she is 21 or older
- Increasing security and bartender detection of fake IDs
- Follow the same procedure when checking each ID; don't be distracted by conversation with the patron
- Check the ID of anyone who looks under the age of 30
- Check the birth date to see that the person is over 21. Check to see if the birth date has been altered
- Check the ID photo and the recorded height for resemblance with the attempted buyer. Compare the hairline, eyebrows and chin shape on the photo-these are the most difficult features to change

- Check the expiration date. If it is expired, it is not a valid ID
- Check the date the ID was issued. The issue date is usually in 4-year increments from the age of 16

- Check the IDs of all people at the bar or table if they all look of questionable age. For example, if a 21-year-old buys a pitcher of beer, check the ID of everyone at the table who appears younger than age 30

- Use UV light to check ID's for 'Secret' UV hologram

If a patron is using a license from another state, compare the license to a representative license from that state. **You can usually obtain a copy of the "United States Driver's Licenses" from your state liquor control board.** Always hold the ID in your hand and feel for any unusual raised surfaces.

NEVER accept or handle a wallet or purse always have the patron remove their ID for your inspection. Look at the ID under a bright light for glue lines or pinholes where bleach may have been injected. See if the format of the card looks correct. Check the font and font type. Check the size, thickness and edges of the ID; ragged edges may indicate tampering. If the word "duplicate" is stamped on the license, someone else may have the original. Ask for another form of identification. Check the back of the ID. On some state licenses, if the numbers have been changed on the front, the true numbers will be shown on the back. If you are unsure, ask for another form of identification or for personal information, such as an address, birth date, age, middle initial, or zodiac sign. **Remember UV light will show hidden 'Secret' holograms, this type of light is inexpensive and invaluable!** If the patron doesn't provide another ID, politely refuse them access to the club and ask them to leave the premises.

Why age identification policies are important for your community
Selling alcohol to people under the age of 21 is illegal. Yet underage youth can easily purchase alcohol with either no age identification or with poor quality fake IDs. In a study conducted in 28 northern Minnesota communities, youthful-looking buyers were able to purchase beer without age identification in 47% of 336 purchase attempts. A study conducted in several New York counties and Washington, D.C. reported that underage buyers were able to purchase alcohol without age identification in 44% to 95% of the purchase attempts.
Although studies show that less than 15% of youths use fake IDs, there are several sources of fake IDs, including:

- Alteration of one's own ID
- Use of someone else's ID, either stolen or borrowed
- Applying for another person's ID using that person's birth certificate
- Creating one's own fake ID
- Purchasing an ID from professional counterfeiters

Servers, clerks, managers and owners of alcohol establishments face the risk of criminal and civil liability if they serve or sell alcohol to an underage person. Checking IDs decreases the potential liability a server or seller could face for selling alcohol to an underage person.

An ID-checking policy also reduces the potential liability of the owners of establishments, who could be sued for illegal alcohol sales that result in an injury to a third party.

* Owners and managers should periodically test their security and staff by having youthful-looking undercover patrons attempt to buy alcohol with no ID or with fake ID.

Policies should also include instructions on what a staff member should do if he/she identifies a fake ID. Guidelines may include:

- Be polite yet firm in refusing the sale to the patron
- Call security
- Confiscate the fake ID when appropriate
- Contact local law enforcement when appropriate
- Establishments may also want to reward employees who confiscate a fake ID, such as giving a small monetary reward of $5-$20 for each ID confiscated.

The Art of Lying

There are numerous ways to detect if someone is lying to you, especially those under age. The majority of the population are not trained to be effective liars, so they usually slip up with one or more of these signs.

Verbal Signs of Lying

- Expand contractions, stressing full-form verbs; such as "did not" and "could not," to convince people they're speaking the truth.

- Deny lying, making emphatic claims to be telling the truth, such as "I have no reason to lie."

- Pause and use non-word sounds during hesitations in their speech ("uh," "er" and "ah" are examples).

- Make speech errors and more frequent mistakes than people who speak the truth. Errors can include grammar, tense and losing thought in mid sentence.

- Stutter, stammer or become tongue-tied.

- Clear their throats and make other noises.

- Use qualifiers and modifiers, explanatory words, such as "however," "sometimes" and "generally."

Nonverbal Signs of Lying:

- Avert their gaze, trying to avoid eye contact.
- Close their hands/interlock their fingers.
- Cross their arms as if creating a barrier.
- Drink and swallow more often than those who tell the truth.
- Use fewer hand gestures, staying stiff, controlling the movements of their hands.
- Shrug their shoulders and flip their hands over in an "open" (palms up) fashion.
- Perform hand-to-face grooming, touching their face, ears and hair.
- Handle objects, such as pens, papers and eyeglasses.
- Blink less than people who tell the truth (just stare at you).

- Do less finger pointing.
- Lean and shift — leaning forward, resting their elbows on desktops or their knees. They also shift often when sitting.
- Lick their lips often.
- Pucker and tighten their lips.
- Sigh and take deep breaths.
- Smile more and laugh inappropriately.
- Touch, scratch and rub their nose frequently.

At last, remember to watch a person's eyes when they are speaking. Often, people who are lying will become shifty eyed or gaze down when telling a lie. Or, they may look to the RIGHT.

Looking to the right indicates they are using the creative side of the brain while looking left indicates MEMORY usage (remembering the past). An easy way to remember this fact is the term, ' Looking Right is Wrong'.

Who do I keep out of the nightclub?

Keeping the nightclub safe means keeping trouble out. Make sure you post outside of the club, a sign explaining the rules & regulations of the establishment. A sign would read like this:

Welcome to the Cooler's Grimoire Nightclub

Dress Code in effect at all times

No torn clothing
No track pants or running suits
No club colors or bandannas
No sleeveless shirts
No sandals

Rules of conduct

No fighting
No aggressive behavior
No selling or using of drugs
No over intoxication
No weapons of any kind

Identification is require to enter this establishment

You must be 21 years of age or older to enter
We except only government issued ID
Back up Id may be required

Failure to meet these rules will result in immediate expulsion from the establishment

Management reserves the right to refuse entry

When working the front door, you are the first line of defense against all sorts of objectionable people. Objectionable people come in all shapes and sizes.

The first type of objectionable person is the intoxicated.

The drunk will often show up on your doorstep, with or without friends. Don't be afraid to turn away a person (and a group) if this is the case. Remember, the law states that it is illegal to be drunk in a public place and it is illegal to serve liquor to a person who is intoxicated. If the liquor inspector comes in and sees a drunk stumbling in your bar, he will ticket you for over-service.

There are levels of intoxication, and you have to decide where to draw the line. If you are not sure if someone is drunk, look for these signs:

- Self-Control & Inhibitions
- Being overly friendly
- Loud speech
- Pace of speech is slow
- Annoying other customers
- Using foul language

Judgment

- Complains about strength of drink
- Changing consumption rate
- Irrational statements
- Buying rounds for strangers
- Complains about prices
- Careless with money

Reason, Caution, Memory

- Starting conversations with strangers
- Making unwanted sexual advances
- Repeating stories and jokes
- Forgetting where they are
- Unable to figure simple calculations

Senses

- Squinting eyes, light sensitivity
- Asking people to speak louder
- Slurring of speech
- Slower response time or the two second delay syndrome
- Eyes unable to follow movement

Coordination & Balance

- Unable to pick up change
- Unable to search for cover charge or money, dropping ID or prolonged searching of wallet,
- Spilling or knocking over drinks
- Swaying, stumbling, bumps into things
- Holds onto chair backs or tables

Vital Centers

- Becomes drowsy, sleepy
- Flush, red face
- Passing out
- Slow, shallow breathing
- Glazed look in eyes

Often people will know that they are drunk but still want to come into your establishment. Look for these signs:

- One friend holding the other up
- One friend distracting you while the other sneaks by
- Talking on the cell phone
- Holding the wall or railing
- Very slow and cautious movement

There are three types of responses when you deny someone entrance into your bar.

- ✓ They will just walk away.
- ✓ They will thank you and walk away.
- ✓ They will become angry and begin to argue/fight with you.

Expect any one of these responses. When you are busy, you don't have time to debate with some overly intoxicated person in your line up at the door. The longer the person hangs around the more patrons it will potentially trouble and the more chances of someone slipping by you. Get them to move along ASAP!

The troublemaker is another type of personality you don't want in your establishment. This especially includes known fighters or patrons who are barred from the establishment. Keep them out.

Large Groups can also pose a problem, especially if you don't know them. Don't be afraid to turn them away or hold onto their IDs when they enter your club. Strangely enough, there is usually a common respect among bouncers, doormen, and/or big guys from other clubs. Most of the time, these people get into the nightclub as VIPs because they are like unpaid staff. The upside to it, is if trouble goes down and your short handed, it's good to have these individuals on your side.

The Biker, depending on whether he is a wannabe or a real hardcore 1%er can cause some possible problems in your establishment. If it's just the local wannabe who likes to play biker on the weekends, no big deal, but if it's a hardcore 1%er, this situation takes a lot of communication skills and experience. It should be conducted with diplomacy and respect at all times. As stated by David L. Hollingworth, owner of nightclubbiz.com:

If you confront gang members in a belligerent manner, then they will no doubt construe it as an act of war – you certainly don't want to do that. If you get the police involved, this could also backfire into a major problem for both you personally, as well as the club. If you want to address the problem peacefully, I strongly suggest diplomacy and not an act of aggression. Yes, you have every right to refuse entrance to anyone you do not deem as desirable, however in this case there may be a cost, and if there is, are you prepared it pay it? If they keep coming in, (which they may very well not), then try to get to know one of the leaders. Trust me; if you show these guys respect, they'll do the same for you. In time, you can nicely approach them with the fact that you enjoy their business, but the colors are intimidating your other customers. Done properly, you can usually work out an agreement. As for your customers, you may loose a few, but believe me, if handled properly it won't be as significant as you may think. They'll get use to it, and life will typically go on. The last thing you want to do is provoke a war on the club or yourself personally.

There are certain groups of individuals that cause more trouble than others. You must know how to profile groups because it saves time and gives you a heads up on potential trouble. The police, FBI and many other organizations use profiling to help them narrow down "suspects". You should do the same. Just ask your cooler about what types of people or groups to look out for, and the old pro will fill you in. You will find more information pertaining to this subject in the Organized Crime chapter. Always remember <u>Public Relations</u>. You want the patrons thinking this: "I had a great time last night. Everyone was in a good mood and there were no fights at the bar." Rather than thinking: "I am never going back to that place. There was a fight and I got knocked over. That place is just trouble." People will always embellish their stories, and this could give the club a bad reputation and damage business. Have a code with the DJ and your security team. If something is happening at the front door and security needs to be called, don't have the DJ say, " All bouncers to the front door!" Make it less conspicuous like," Code blue - area one." Contained discretion works the best. Always put the nightclub you work at in a good light. You want the patrons coming back to your club and they certainly don't want to hang out at a rough bar. The type of bar you have will dictate what type of patrons you attract. Fights attract fighters! That is why it is important to set the right tempo for your nightclub and maintain policy to keep it running smoothly.

So to summarize this chapter we accept only 4 types of IDs:

- ❖ **Passport**
- ❖ **Provincial or State Drivers License**
- ❖ **Provincial or State ID card**
- ❖ **Military ID**

We ask the following questions:

- ✓ Ask the person their date of birth.
- ✓ Ask for their birth sign.
- ✓ Ask what their address is.
- ✓ Ask for other back up IDs, such as a birth certificate.

We check for:
- ✓ Check their photo.
- ✓ Check height.
- ✓ Check to see if the ID/DL is expired.
- ✓ If needed - do a signature check.
- ✓ Use UV and LED light to check holograms

Chapter Seven:

Working the Floor

Once the master is gone..

That which has been learned becomes priceless…

Ivan 'Doc' Holiday

The Art of Working the Floor

When working the floor one must be alert and quick thinking. The floor is not consistent, it is unpredictable as patrons interact and walk about, leave and enter the nightclub/bar. The nightclub security professional must adapt to the movement and the patron flow. The security monitors the patrons, the staff members and the property. Examples of this would be as follows:

- Watching patrons for aggressive or unruly behavior.
- Watching for overly intoxicated patrons.
- Watching for drug dealers or prostitutes.
- Watching for staff members stealing.
- Watching for bartenders over pouring or giving away free drinks.
- Watching for fires.
- Watching for patrons or staff destroying property.
- Watching for damage and flooding in the bathrooms.

The list is endless for what a bouncer/doorman must keep a watchfully eye out for. Some clubs can have any number of patrons. For example when this author worked at the Broken Spoke Saloon in Sturgis, South Dakota- the biggest biker bar in the world, it was not uncommon to have 5000 patrons per night during the one-week event.

It is important to have the appropriate 'Patrons to Security' ratio. But there is a catch-22 here, there is no point in hiring twenty bouncers and only ten are any good. It is important to hire **quality not quantity**. People that work the door are the first line of defense against under age drinkers and other undesirables. They are the gatekeepers. The people who work the floor are the enforcers of club regulations as well as the laws of the city, county, and the state. The floor security check ID's in the event that a minor gets past the door security. They watch for potential problems from aggressive and/or overly intoxicated customers. They protect fellow employees, club property and provide a safe environment for the club's patrons. Security personnel who work the floor must make sure that the club's employees and customers are not buying, selling or using drugs. They must ensure that employees and customers are not stealing from the club or each other. They must make sure that prostitution or other sexual activities do not take place in the club or on the property. **It is the responsibility of the floor security to know where all First Aid kits are located and the location of all the fire extinguishers.** They must keep all stairways, entrances and exits as well as all walkways, free of patrons who might block these areas, preventing people from exiting club in an emergency. Security strategy should include door, roaming, and stationary security as well as supervisors or coolers. Coolers or supervisors have the responsibility to make sure all security personnel are properly trained and posted to produce maximum efficiency and security. The cooler is the chief of security. He has the final say in all matters of security that arise. His job is to control his security staff, defuse volatile situations and to determine if customers involved in a situation may stay or be asked to leave the club. He is the leader and must lead by example. He must be calm, objective and emotionally detached at all times. The cooler must be regarded as a confident person of authority by his co-workers and patrons. The security personnel will follow the cooler's lead. If he is hot headed, aggressive or indecisive they will respond in a similar manner. The cooler must remain calm having the ability to make quick evaluations and proper decisions. The cooler must conduct him or herself in a professional manner at all times. This ensures that the other security personnel will confidently follow his example. His decision is final, non negotiable, and must be followed without question. Today most establishments incorporate a "No hands Policy", therefore, the days of bouncers intimidating, manhandling, and beating up patrons as an acceptable practice are long gone. If club security and owners do not grasp the reality that this type of behavior is both illegal and immoral they are opening themselves up to lawsuits and bad publicity. Security personnel who cannot operate within legal guidelines should be terminated or forced to resign. Club owners are responsible for the actions of their employee's and vice versa. A club being sued can run into high legal fees, increased insurance rates and/or even loss of their liquor license. In addition the club can receive bad publicity, which will cause good customers to stay away

from the club and go to other clubs where they feel safer. To complicate matters clubs with violent reputations attract people who look forward to violent confrontations with club security and other patrons. These actions will lead to a non-stop cycle of police complaints as well as insurance carriers refusing to provide liability insurance at a reasonable price, if they even offer it at all.

Club security should NEVER engage in or initiate unnecessary fights.

If attempts to peacefully defuse a situation fail and it escalates to a physical confrontation, we use the techniques of contain, restrain and remove, using the minimal force necessary to expel the problem from the club. If security personnel follow this procedure it will save the club owner thousands of dollars in litigation fees. If they insist on using old school tactics, such as punching, kicking and fighting, the club will pay, and pay plenty! It is in a club's best interest to conduct background checks on staff members, to ensure that violent felons and criminals are not hired. In most cases criminal background checks can be completed in less that 24 hours and at a price of about $20 per bouncer.
If possible have your security personnel certified by a reputable nightclub security training program.

Stationary vs. Roaming

The stationary bouncer will see more than the roaming bouncer. Reason being, the roaming bouncer must watch not only for trouble but where he/she is walking. Thus the stationary security professional can remain still and visually monitor the crowd, using both his/her Central vision and Peripheral vision (Side vision). The ability to see objects and movement outside of the direct line of vision is a great benefit to the bouncer/doorman. Peripheral vision is the work of the rods, nerve cells located largely outside the macula (the center) of the retina.

The rods are also responsible for night vision and low-light vision but are insensitive to color, as opposed to central vision. Nightclub/bar security should implement both stationary and roaming security. The roaming security should be the Cooler (chief of security) and the more experienced security personnel. The Cooler is able to roam about observing his security team and making position changes as the crowd dictates. The cooler will engage in shadowing and probing the crowd for signs of unseen trouble. The cooler is always ready to assist the security team and direct them. He is the person of authority when pertaining to security matters. Stationary security are usually located on high-stands or in an area that places them above the crowd. This gives the stationary bouncer the ability to monitor a large crowd with a wide-ranging field of both central and peripheral vision. They can also keep track and touch base with security team members. A considerable advantage is the ability to watch bartenders, waitresses and other members of the staff. The stationary security professional can relay unseen trouble to the team and leave the stand to assist. The only draw back is having stationary placements that are too high and thus hard to get down from in a hurry. But given that, an equal balance of roaming and stationary security would be the best system.

The no-hands policy methodology.
The no-hands policy is simply an establishment that does not want any patron physically removed unless security is forced to defend themselves or others from physical violence. Thus the routine is straightforward, you conduct business as usual following the SAR Matrix and De-escalation techniques in the previous chapter.

* When removing violent patrons always use the closest Exit. Avoid front door removal if possible to protect incoming patrons.

In the author's first book 'The Bouncer's Bible' - Three factors are vital to the art of bouncing: **Teamwork, Communication, and Position.**

Teamwork

Aside from any required technical proficiency, a wide variety of social skills are desirable for successful teamwork, including:

- The ability to follow the chain of command.
- The ability to work with others for the good of the team.
- Listening - it is important to listen to other team member's views. When people are allowed to freely express their ideas, these initial ideas will produce other ideas.
- Questioning - it is important to ask questions, interact, and discuss the objectives of the security team. Brainstorming creates new ideas.
- Respect - it is important to treat others with respect and to support their ideas. Respect is never given - it is earned.
- Assistance - it is crucial to support one's team members, which is the general premise of teamwork.
- Openness - it is important to share security related matters with the team to create an environment of collaborative teamwork.
- Participation - all members of the staff are encouraged to participate in any matters that involve the security team.

Communication

For a security team to work effectively it is essential that team members acquire communication skills and use effective communication channels between one another using voice, security radios, hand signals, report writing, group meetings and so on. This will enable team members to work together and achieve their overall goal and objective. Communication is not only the ability to stay in contact but the ability to understand and value the true brotherhood of bouncing. Brotherhood in bouncing is formed very much like a friendship or family. The team bonds out of respect for each member's skill and support. As time passes the team grows stronger ties as members support and help each other. A hierarchy develops based on time, experience, knowledge and respect.

Position

This is a very important factor in the security team equation. Simply put it is **being in the right place at the right time!** But this can only be accomplished if one knows when and where to move. The cooler positions his team in locations that will best correspond with the crowd. On an individual level, a bouncer will position him or herself so as to be able to watch the largest number of patrons and react swiftly should a problem arise.

It is very much like chess, one positions his pieces to best defend and strike. However, what pieces he moves will also be dictated by the play of his opponent. Thus, as the nightclub/bar crowd moves and gathers in different areas, so the security team reposition themselves for maximum efficiency.

Security personnel may take up positions next to a group of patrons displaying aggressive behavior or in a section of the club that is prone to prohibited activities.   When dealing with unruly patrons, always try to talk the customer out of your club; NEVER engage in unnecessary physical force. Treat each customer the way you would want to be treated if you were in his or her position. **When dealing with undesirables remember, it is easier to keep them out, than to put them out.** When your team has to remove an unruly patron, work together and support your team members. If any of them are erroneous in their judgment or procedure, complete the removal, promote teamwork and organize a security meeting after hours to discuss and resolve the issue. Never disagree in public, do not show dissension or confusion. Always present a unified solidarity to the public. Never embarrass a patron, always try to let him or her save face and try to leave him or her an out. Don't insult or belittle them, putting them in a corner where they feel the need to fight to save their honor. In the event of an incident never respond alone, always have backup when possible. Don't crowd the customer but let him see you have team backup so that he understands that if he chooses to be combative he will not win! NEVER have security respond to a situation, as though they were all members of an attacking barbarian horde, all leaving their posts, running through the club, knocking over tables and customers in order to respond to a problem! It looks foolish, it is unprofessional and unsafe! We protect our patrons not trample them!

In regards to removing unruly female patrons, nothing will start a bar room brawl faster than a gorgeous intoxicated female kicking and screaming for help! This is a sexual assault charge waiting to happen and surrounding male patrons are quick to fight to save the honor of a damsel in distress!

Be smart and be careful when dealing with unruly females.

* <u>Show up in full force – Follow protocol – Remove the problem!</u>

When having to deal with family members in your club, NEVER get involved in a Domestic Conflict. Any police officer will tell you, they dread having to respond to a domestic violence call. **They are unpredictable and dangerous.** Family members will fight among themselves, but when confronted will stand together and attack a common foe.

The nightclub security professional responds the same way to family feuds in the nightclub/bar as with unruly female patrons.

Be smart and be careful when dealing with feuding family members.

*<u>Show up in full force – Follow protocol – Remove the problem!</u>

Doc Holiday & son Caine workin the Roadhog Saloon, NH in 2000

Band and Dance floor areas.

Dance floors are areas that initiate fights in most clubs. The reason being, you have individuals moving and sometimes banging into each other. In some establishments such as Rave or Punk Rock clubs patrons 'Slam Dance' and physically run into each other. Thus the dance floor can be a vigorous place and needs to be monitored with stationary security. The following are some basic guidelines:

- No drinks should be allowed on the dance floor.
- No lit cigarettes or open fire.
- No aggressive or offensive dance moves.
- No dancing on the bar, on tables or on hazardous objects. (Example: chairs or speakers) remember the club's liability insurance!!
- Watch for smaller patrons falling or getting stepped on.
- Watch for overly- intoxicated or drugged up patrons
- Watch for prohibited sexual acts

In many clubs, security will be responsible for the safety of bands and their equipment, as well as areas designated for band use. I recommend that stationary security be posted on opposite sides of the stage, positioned so that they can watch the crowd with a view unobstructed by equipment or bright spotlights. Post a bouncer/doorman at the entrance of the backstage area to prevent unauthorized people from gaining access.

In addition one or two bouncers will provide band security on the floor in front of stage. NEVER let people on the stage, near the equipment or backstage unless they are wearing visible band/guest back stage passes. Security should also be prepared to stop band members from committing illegal acts or safety code violations such as using illegal pyrotechnics, illicit drugs, diving into the crowd or throwing objects at the audience. The dance floor is secured in a similar manner as the stage, you post several stationary security personnel, and at least two roaming bouncers to observe the dancers and remove bottles, glass and other objects from the dance floor in order to ensure the safety of the dancers. Other assignments would be to watch for drunken patrons or aggressive dancers who constantly are bumping into other customers. Security should also watch for groping of females or sexually suggestive activities. Your response will however depend on what the club management deems appropriate behavior.

Billiard Area

The billiard area or pool table area is in my opinion, one of the most dangerous areas in a nightclub or bar. There are many opportunities for problems to arise from excessive drinking and/or drugs, poor sportsmanship, cheating, illegal gambling, side bets and so forth. They have easy access to readily available weapons such as pool cues, and pool balls, both which can be used with deadly results. Pool balls are dangerous projectiles when thrown and pool cues can be used as a bludgeon. Security should remember this when confronting an angry patron holding a pool cue.

Beware if a violent patron is holding the pool cue with the larger heavy end facing you! **In survival mode: Pool balls hit harder than pool cues!** Regardless of the outcome never turn your back to a patron with a pool cue! Alertness is the secret to billiard area security, being aware of your surroundings. It is vital that when security is directed to the billiard area that they assert control immediately! If arguing ensues or equipment is being abused, you must issue a firm, respectful warning, advising that if this behavior continues the billiard area will be shut down and patrons will be asked to leave the club or expel them from the club immediately. Once you have issued the warning, be prepared to enforce your decision, never second guess yourself, make the call and stick to it, if you don't it will only come back to haunt you later!

VIP and Private Areas

Many clubs have VIP and private areas, off limits to the general public, unless an entry fee is paid or they are there by invitation only. The only complicated VIP areas are in the Strip Clubs. Strip clubs always have these rooms, used to provide the dancer and a patron with a private area to conduct their business. By business, I mean 'private lap dances'. A security camera monitors this area with a stationary bouncer there at all times to ensure dancer safety and lawful conduct. In other establishments
these areas are relatively simple to secure, requiring a door person to secure the entrance and be in contact with the team should a problem arise. It is important to realize that sometimes certain customers will become offended and agitated when they find out that these areas are

off limits to them. I have seen pleasant customers become belligerent, when they believe that you are denying them access to these areas, because "they are not good enough", or "their being stereotyped"
This is the time when your patience and people skills will be tested. Be professional, remain calm and attempt to reason with the customer. Sometimes, I will try to smooth the customer's ruffled feathers by having "the house" buy him and his guests a round of drinks. I may also have the customer revisit the club at another date and waive the cover charge. Remember, in this situation…patience is a virtue!

Bathrooms and Backrooms

In every club that I have ever worked in, it is the responsibility of security to oversee these areas. These areas are the ones that seem to invite more than their fair share of problems. These are the areas that seem to invite fights, sexual acts, drug use, drug sales and destruction of club property. Check these areas often and follow these guidelines:

- **Always be on your guard! Many muggings and assaults occur in these areas**
- **Have backup when checking these areas**
- **Expect the unexpected**
- **Never overlook any illegal activities. If you see them, stop them, have the wrongdoers leave the club and if necessary call the police.**
- **Try to keep track of who enters and exits these areas**

The Parking Lot   a.k.a. 'The Asphalt Arena'

This is a critical area for any club, most assaults and muggings occur in this area. Customer and employee vehicles are prone to being broken into or vandalized. Acts of prostitution will take place in dark area's and parked vehicles. Many drug deals are transacted in the parking areas. More sexual assaults will occur in the parking lot than in any other area of the club. Bouncers nickname the parking lots "Asphalt Arena's" because it is where most fights take place. Back in the old days, fights that started in the club were taken outside and finished in the parking lot. Many of the fights were started by security! So what can security do to make the parking lot safer? Suggest to management that brighter lights be used in the parking area also suggest that video cameras and monitors be used to provide constant surveillance to compliment security foot patrols through the parking lot. When checking the parking area, always stagger the patrol times. Enter and leave the parking lot from different approaches, do not be predictable! Be alert, look for anything out of place, if something looks wrong, investigate with caution. Make sure to check between the parked cars and inside of the cars. If there are storage areas, make sure the doors are locked and secured. Utilize a flashlight and either a radio system to communicate with your security team, or a cell phone to call the police, fire department or an ambulance. **Always escort females, elderly or handicapped patrons to their vehicles, they present an inviting target to potential criminals**. Your customers will appreciate it, and tell others that you operate a safe establishment. If a fight breaks out in your club, you must extract the aggressive patrons. However, do not let them continue their brawl in the parking lot! Go out and stop it, call the police if necessary.

Leaving the Club

For club personnel, this can be the most dangerous time. Potential thieves, rapists, stalkers and drunken angry customers may be waiting to ambush the unaware off-duty employee. When leaving the club, observe the area, be aware of people loitering around the area and parked vehicles that do not belong there. Try to leave together, make sure everyone gets in his or her vehicles. I always escort each female to their vehicle, wait for them to lock their doors and drive away. At that point all males enter their vehicles and leave parking lot together, never leaving anyone alone. If you have a tactical baton or pepper spray. Have it ready, you never know when you will be forced to use it! Remember, angry customers who were put out of the club have confronted many bar employees in the parking lot. Any person knows that if you work at a club, you may have a vehicle in the parking lot. <u>Never</u> leave personal information in your vehicle that identifies you or your family. Example: you have your cell phone bill sitting on the dash of your car. A rapist sees it and gets your home address and phone number.

Be Alert! Never divulge personal information to persons you do not know in the club.

Money Drops

Club security is often called upon to make money drops or pickups. There are several types of money transactions. Security may be required to move money from cash register to cash register or pickup excess cash and place it in a secure area or safe. When making bank drops after hours, I vary my routes, watch for being followed, use multiple cars and circle the bank to get a total picture of the area. Be aware of dimly lit areas, trees or shrubbery that could conceal a potential robber! Watch for parked cars or people loitering in the area. If it does not feel right, leave. If need be call the police to provide backup. Always trust your instincts! A little common sense and preparation can reduce the likelihood that you will become a victim.

Final Thoughts

The preceding points are observations that I have made over the years. Use them and make them part of your security profession.   It is important to remember that you and your job must have unified principles, meaning you have to be morally comfortable with your job and its requirements. If you are not, you will have to compromise your principles or find another job.

Document everything, fill out daily reports in a security log, that way you protect the bar and yourself. If there is ever a legal question concerning an incident, it is necessary that you have all documented information available for police and/or legal investigators in the event of criminal or civil complaints. "Distraction is the enemy of attention" Doc once told me. I always keep in mind the "Ten Commandments of Bouncing", from the book 'The Bouncer's Bible', written by my good friend and mentor Ivan "Doc" Holiday

1- **No one ever wins a fight.**

2- **Know yourself.**

3- **Expect the unexpected.**

4- **Never underestimate anyone.**

5- **Never lose control.**

6- **Respect everyone.**

7- **Have compassion and understanding for others.**

8- **Never speak ill of others.**

9- **Never touch alcohol or drugs when working.**

10- **Never take things personal, remember…it's just a job!**

Rockin Mel Cardonell & Ivan 'Doc' Holiday

Chapter Eight:

Organized Crime

Power tends to corrupt, and absolute power corrupts absolutely.

Lord Acton, Letter to Bishop Mandell Creighton, 1887

Organized Crime

As this author knows only to well, if you spend enough years working in the nightclub security industry, sooner or later you will come across some form of Organized Crime. In years past, I have personally headed security at clubs owned by OC (Organized Crime). 'Trial by fire' is a dangerous but valuable learning tool. OC members can be patrons, silent partners in the club or owners of the establishment. OC members have diverse personalities. But remember this, a Black Mamba can have a well-behaved disposition and/or it can have a fearsome temperament...but the fact remains, it is still a Deadly Snake! Fool around with it long enough and you are going to get a strike. OC members should be dealt with in the same manner. OC members are unpredictable, calculated and dangerous. They have a mindset based solely on a 'Tribal Mentality'. Remember what we covered in the first chapter regarding the Tribal Mentality - *"A modern example of the tribal mentality would be Organized Crime in form of street gangs, motorcycle gangs, prison gangs, Mafias, Cartels...etc. A cycle of violence and tribal war can take place between two ordinary people and their families, or two heads of states, or two gang leaders who perceive each other as enemies or potential threat. As the war continues both enemies pass on their tribal mindset to the next generation who, once brainwashed, join the tribal war started by their elders and previous generations."*

OC members are all about their business and their brotherhood. Anyone who interferes with either one is looking for severe tribulations. A bouncer/doorman must always be alert and watching for this type of potentially dangerous patron. Thus is the reason for this chapter. The nightclub security professional must be able to identify a genuine OC gang member from a person who dresses the part and talks a lot of smack. You are going to get the wannabe bikers, wise guys and GITs (gangster-in-training). You have to decipher the real deal from the impersonator. Education is the key. **Knowledge is power.**

The History of Gangs

Since biblical times criminal organizations that engage in secretive, anti-social and criminal behavior has continued to plague society. These criminal groups have been apart of history for thousands of years and their roots run deep into America's past and culture. Gangs are not a new phenomenon nor are the problems associated with them, however, they have never touched a greater segment of society as they do now. The birth of America's gang problem can be traced to the dawn of the country, a time when many Europeans migrated to the East coast with the intent of making a better life. After arriving, their savings were quickly depleted and many were forced to take out loans with local merchants and colonization companies, who charged steep interest rates. Life for many was more difficult than they imagined and death due to poverty and disease was common.

There were many who died orphaning their children. With no money to send the children back to their homeland and with no relatives to care for them in America, this became a common problem in many cities.

1700 - 1790s:

During the mid-1700s most towns had an orphanage managed by the local church. Even cities with populations as small as 1,000 people had an orphanage. Most families had their own trials and tribulations and to worry about someone else's children was just too much to expect. As a result adoptions were rare. Children wandering the streets was so common that the orphanage's philosophy was to keep the children separated from the rest of society, not to find a home for them. With little funding and no operational rules or guidelines, children housed in these institutions lived in despicable conditions. To better prepare the children for entering society an apprentice program was created which could be described as the predecessor to the country's foster care programs. Starting as early as 10-years-old, a boy was taken out of the orphanage and placed with the local blacksmith, butcher, shopkeeper or with someone who could teach him a trade. The boy was taught a trade and received food and shelter. In exchange, the business owner had an employee at a fraction of the cost of hiring an adult. It was hoped that once the boy entered manhood, he would start his own business and become a productive member of society. In reality, community leaders found that the boys were receiving little care and guidance. They quickly discovered that after the boys completed their daily chores, they received no additional supervision or guidance.

Juvenile delinquency became a major concern as scores of homeless children strolled the streets in nearly every large city. Children and teenagers stealing food and clothing was a common problem. Night watchmen had difficulty keeping the youngsters from engaging in minor acts of mischief. Although the youth were banded together, they were more of a nuisance for the communities rather than feared violent organizations. Crime rates quickly rose and by 1790, slave labor was in such abundance that the apprentice program was abandon.

1791 – 1849:

As residents of the country were burdened with heavy taxes, organized smuggling and robbery gangs were found in every major coastal city. These adult gangs such as the Doane Gang were known for committing vicious acts of robbery. The Doane Gang existed for nearly 10 years until they were caught and executed. In 1791 gangs were such a problem that city officials in Philadelphia had an emergency meeting to decide how to deal with their city's gang problem. They determined they had numerous groups of disruptive youth engaged in organized criminal acts. The early 1800s brought a definite distinction in social classes and the gang problem continued to grow touching all age groups. Gangs were generally comprised of members of the same race and ethnic background, who banded together for protection, recreation and financial gain. In Manhattan, the Forty Thieves Gang operated as professional murderers, muggers, burglars, and pickpockets. Their younger auxiliary, the Little Forty Thieves Gang was soon created which consisted of juvenile delinquents as young as 10-years-old.

In 1825, the Little Forty Thieves Gang and the many other youth gangs caused New York City officials to announce their city had a gang problem.

1850 - 1860:

By the 1850's, gangs such as the Plug Uglies Gang, the Dead Rabbits Gang and the Chichesters Gang were formed. The Plug Uglies Gang received their name from the giant plug hats they wore. The hats were filled with rags, wool and leather and were worn over their ears as helmets to protect them during gang fights. They required all members to be of Irish decent and to be at least 6 feet tall. The Dead Rabbits Gang specialized in mugging, pick pocketing and robbery. This gang existed for nearly twenty years and was known to carry a spear with a dead rabbit mounted on it during all conflicts with rival groups. The Chichesters Gang got their name from their homeland, a city in Ireland. The gang problem was virtually described as an Irish and Welsh problem. For many years Irish, Welsh and Chinese immigrants migrated to the country and were used as a source of cheap labor. The Chinese moved into communities and quickly isolated themselves from the American culture. Tong and Triad groups quickly formed in every Chinese-American community. Criminal groups controlled by the Chinese received little attention from the media, but they were credited with bringing opium into the country. It was the Irish gangs who had membership numbers in the thousands and it was they who received all the attention in the media. In large cities gang membership continued to increase until the gangs gained powerful control over many neighborhoods. As citizens became more concerned, government officials blamed unwed mothers and the perils of illegitimacy as the cause of their increasing gang problems.

This 1850s report was unsurprisingly familiar to a 1989 report by the U. S. House Committee. The committee blamed the breakdown of the family structure as the cause of violence in a statement released to the New York Times. It was not until 1853 that a New York City police captain organized the Strong Arm Squad to combat their growing gang problem. The squad consisted of the bravest and strongest men who daily assaulted and arrested gang members whether or not they were currently engaged in criminal activity.

1861 - 1869

Problems continued to increase until the beginning of the Civil war in 1861. At the end of the war in 1865, the founding year of the Ku Klux Klan, gang problems rapidly resurfaced. Former members of the Chichesters Gang created the Whyos Gang. They consisted of several hundred members and were believed to be the most vicious and terrifying of the time. They were so brazen in their criminal activity that they printed up a list of services, "Punching - $2, Both Eyes Blackened - $4, Nose & Jaw Broken - $10, Jacked Out (knocked out with a blackjack) - $15, Ear Chewed Off - $15, Leg Or Arm Broken - $19, Shot in The Leg - $25, Stab - $25, Doing the Job (murder) $100 and up." Several years later the gang required all prospective members to have committed a murder before receiving admission into the group. Following the Civil War many soldiers returned home addicted to morphine because of their wartime injuries. Drug abuse was a common problem among young and old. Most gangs recognized the needs of the public and quickly took advantage of the demand for drugs. There was easy access to morphine, cocaine and laudanum; a popular depressant.

These drugs quickly stripped away what little values, ethics or remorse that a gang member had. Jacob Reiss, a photographer and journalist of the time, documented an incident in which two members of the Montgomery Guards Gang were arrested for murder.

Reiss said that after the two young suspects robbed a Jewish peddler; they bragged how they tried to cut off the victim's head. When questioned about the attempted decapitation, the suspects smugly replied that it was "just for fun."

1870 - 1890

The first Boys Club of America was founded in 1870 to help "pavement children" like the young members of the 'Nineteenth Street Gang'.
The 'All Catholic' gang had the

reputation of preying on shopkeepers, disabled people, and children. The gang, consisting of all teenagers under 16-years-old, was blamed for several attacks on Protestant missions and schools. As gangs continued to expand in inner-city areas, membership in rural areas grew as well. It was during this time the government recognized the need of a law enforcement organization that would span the entire nation. Shortly later, the Federal Bureau of Investigation started with just one employee. In 1887 the Red Sash Gang was notorious for numerous acts of murder and cattle rustling. Each member of the gang wore a red sash to show their affiliation to the group. That same year the Burrows Gang robbed dozens of trains and stagecoaches.

1891 – 1899

In the summer of 1895 in the Arkansas-Oklahoma territory, Rufus Buck and his friends started a gang. The young teens began their criminal reign with the murder of a deputy sheriff who they believed was looking at them suspiciously. They later found a widowed woman and after gang-raping her, they killed her. The young teens then did a home invasion robbery. After raping the woman of the home, they murdered her husband and children. The gang was soon caught after a shootout with police, and were later hung.

1900 - 1910

In the early 1900s, keeping up with technological advances, the organization level of gangs took a dramatic increase. In one city, the Car Barn Gang posted a sign on every street-corner reading, *"Notice-COPS, KEEP OUT! No policemen will hereafter be allowed on this block. By order of the Car Barn Gang."*

They had such control of the neighborhood that police had to move through the streets in squads of at least six men to avoid showers of bricks and attacks from gang members. Patrolmen who did enter this forbidden area were commonly stabbed or beaten with blackjacks. By the early 1900s, Irish citizens were no longer considered second-class citizens and Italian and Jewish controlled gangs were in nearly every large city. Gangs were no longer just a problem among the Irish community. Drunkenness and immorality plagued the entire country.

1911 - 1920

Drug abuse was a familiar problem in all large cities and to combat the growing drug addiction among the population the Harrison Narcotic Act was signed in March of 1915. This began the government's first attempt at regulating narcotics. Within five years the Volstead Act was announced and 'prohibition' began, making the production and use of all alcoholic beverages illegal. Again, the concept of supply and demand was recognized and many gangs went into the business of producing and selling liquor.

1921 - 1929

Known as the Golden Era of Gangs, the roaring twenties produced the

most notorious criminals ever known, such as Alphonse "Scarface" Capone, Charles "Pretty Boy" Floyd and John Dillinger. Italian crime syndicates monopolized the criminal world and Chicago became the new home of the country's gang problem.

A special law enforcement organization was created and agents were issued a badge, grenades, a machine gun, a .45 caliber pistol with an extra magazine, and 3,000 rounds of ammunition. These agents were better equipped than most law enforcement officers of today. Eventually the Italian controlled crime groups merged into one large organization known as the mafia, whose members called their group "La Cosa Nostra" or "This thing of ours". Although the country's fascination focused on these organized crime groups, youth gangs were still a problem in all large cities and nearly every one of these groups were involved in the illegal production and distribution of liquor. Youth gangs such as the Big Boom Gang was identified. The Big Boom Gang was known for using BB guns and shotguns loaded with rock salt during fights with rival gangs and the police.

1930 - 1949

During the1930s the F. B. I. began collecting and tabulating crime

reports from across the nation.
Social workers began their
campaign after recognizing the
problem of youth's running the
streets. Their solution was to
produce a movie called The Dead
End. Their goal was to show teens
the perils of a life on the streets.

Although the success or failure of the film was never mentioned, with
the declaration of World War II several years later gang membership
levels once again dwindled. Throughout the war, racial tension
increased in many parts of the country and following the example of the
prior Irish, Jewish, and Italian groups. Mexican gangs became more
organized. In Los Angeles, the Zoot Suit Riots occurred after
community leaders and military personnel focused their attention toward
the growing number of Mexican-Americas who called themselves
Pachucos. During this time, many innocent Mexican-American citizens
were targeted in unjustified attacks and false arrests. At the end of the
war in 1945, solders returned to their homes and displaced many
women and minorities from their jobs causing the poverty and
unemployment level to increase in many inner-city areas.

1950 - 1960

By 1950 the United States has the worst juvenile crime statistics in the Western world. Three years later, New York started the first youth curfew and warned defiant teens to expect to have their "skulls cracked" if found out past curfew. In several cities young Black men formed social organizations and rivalries quickly became apparent between many of these groups. Although many of the groups began for racial and social advancement, violent criminal activity soon followed and these groups became the seedlings for some of the most notorious gangs the nation has ever known. Within the same decade organized prison gangs were formed and across the country drug use took a dramatic increase.

The next thirty years brought many gangs who focused their efforts toward the manufacturing, distributing and trafficking of controlled substances.

At the beginning of the civil rights movement in the mid-1960s, gang-related violence continued to increase to unprecedented levels. Many of the gangs formed during this time are still in existence today ending the supremacy of one racial group controlling organized crime.

The gang problem now belongs to everyone-Asian, Black, Hispanic, and White. Gangsters of all races now share the underworld. The social and economical burden that gang members inflict upon society is not a new problem.

Gang rapes, drive-by shootings, home invasion robberies and murders have been commonplace for hundreds of years. Although they may have ridden horses instead of cars, wore hats instead of bandanas and carried knives instead of automatic weapons, gangs are not a new tribulation facing the citizenry of this country. Since the beginning of civilization, gangs in one degree or another have always contributed to the decay of society and although the United States is the most technological advanced nation in the world, the gang problem continued to grow faster than any virus or disease.

AN OVERVIEW OF STREET GANGS - PRESENT DAY

Generally, for purposes of this discussion, a gang can be considered to be a loosely organized group of individuals who collaborate together for social reasons. Modern day gangs now collaborate together for anti-social reasons. Gangs generally have a leader or group of leaders who issue orders and reap the fruits of the gang's activities. A gang may also wear their "colors", wear certain types of clothing, tattoos, brands, or likewise imprint their gang's name, logo, or other identifying marks on their bodies. Many gangs also adopt certain types of hairstyles and communicate through the use of hand signals and graffiti on walls, streets, schoolwork, and school property. It must be understood that it is not illegal to be in a gang and indeed many adults are currently involved in activities that meet Webster's definition for a gang.

However, many gangs of today, especially youthful gangs, break the law to provide funding for gang activities or to further the gang's reputation on the streets. Gangs may identify with a large city gang or remain locally turf oriented. Development of local intelligence as well as pro-active events are a mandatory part of dealing with this problem. Schools must develop lines of communication with law enforcement officials in order to track and prevent gang growth and violence effectively. Over the last several years in Arkansas, gangs have made an evolution from being turf and brotherhood oriented to now being involved in one way or another with criminal enterprises. Some sell drugs, some steal cars, some brutalize and rob, and some do all of the above. Local gang members have stated that out of town connections many times bring in guns and drugs from other communities for distribution. Groups that may have started out as a delinquent band of neighborhood toughs have now turned into a violent drug gang, some of whom retain a gang identity for enforcement, collection, or other reasons. Most gang members crave power, or "juice" as it is known in gang slang. Several years ago, a pecking order within a gang may have been established by flying fists. Now it is settled by flying lead. Joining a group known to have a reputation, good or bad, gives a kid looking for a purpose, something to belong to. Participants have said the mere interaction of members, listening to one another's problems and sharing the other trials and tribulations today's teens are faced with are the drawing card for them to become a banger. Gang members also claim to enjoy the respect or fear others exhibit around them. Then they say, the money begins flowing, and with that comes all of the things associated with material wealth that is usually beyond the reach of those adolescents without the criminal activity of being involved in a gang.

All of this is quite a heady trip for a young kid. Once a kid gets into a gang, over and over they are told there is no way out. They fear serious reprisals from fellow gang members if a defection is suspected. Some are told they will be killed if they try to get out. Others are told that they can kill their mother to earn their way out. You must remember when dealing with a kid involved in this that our beliefs must be set aside because the young person's beliefs are what we are dealing with, and you can bet that they believe everything the gang tells them. Sociologists as well as gang members have isolated the following reasons for joining a street gang:

Identity	Discipline
Recognition	Love
Belonging	Money

Additionally, many kids are intimidated into gangs to avoid continued harassment. Gangs provide their members and family members with protection from other gangs as well as any other perceived threats. Little Rock gangs have been highly noticeable since about 1988. Prior to that time, there were neighborhood gangs of various groups, both black and white, reported in and around Little Rock. These groups were mainly social in nature and did not crave the same things our current batch of gangsters appear to be wanting. The current gang structure became increasingly visible at a time that paralleled the introduction of crack cocaine to the streets.

Gang culture is also highly glamorized by the media including television, big screen releases, and powerful, idolized hard-core rap artists who rap about revolutions and killing. This music is in great demand by both white and black kids and provides the role models for many of the dress habits and slang of today's street culture. Gangs are nothing new. Many large police departments on the east coast had gang units at the turn of the century to monitor the mainly immigrant gangs who protected their neighborhoods and came together for social reasons. Gangs, as most people think of them, probably began to be recognized by the general public around the nation with the birth of the Los Angeles gangs in the early seventies. Gang-like activity has actually plagued large cities around the nation for years. In Los Angeles, the average age of a gang member is around 25 years old while Arkansas gang members still appear in their teens. Older individuals sometimes claim gang membership for similar reasons as teens. Recently, street graffiti was found that indicated second-generation membership in a local street gang. Feelings of fear, hatred, bigotry, poverty, disenfranchisement, and the general breakdown of social values are also considered motivations for joining a street group.

Even though we have currently identified about forty different named gangs in the local area, they all appear to align with four large major city gangs:

- **Crips - L.A. oriented**
- **Bloods - L.A. oriented**
- **Folk Nation - a/k/a Hoovers, BGD's, Shorty Folks, Shorties**
                                                    -Chicago oriented
- **People Nation - a/k/a Vice Lords, P Stone Rangers, Blackstone,Rangers, Latin Kings-Chicago oriented**

Gangs will sometimes change affiliations. It must always be remembered that gangs are very fluid in nature and changes occur almost daily. That again points to the importance of developing local skill in monitoring the growth and movement of the groups.

In order to better understand the gang mentality, the following are considered the "Three R's" of gang culture:

(1) REPUTATION / REP - This is of critical concern to "gangbangers" (gang members). A rep extends not only to each individual, but also to the gang as a whole. In some groups, status (or rank) is gained within the gang by having the most "juice" based largely on one's reputation. While being "juiced" is very important, the manner by which the gang member gains the "juice" is just as important. Upon interview, many gang members embellish their past gang activities in an attempt to impress their conversation partner.

Gang members freely admit crimes and it has been my experience that most in fact do embellish their stories to enhance their feeling of power. In many gangs, to become a member, you must be "jumped in" by members of the gang. This entails being "beaten down" until the leader calls for it to end. Afterwards, all gang members hug one another to further the "G thing". This action is meant to bond the members together as a family. Frequently, young gang members, whether hardcore or associate, will talk of fellowship and the feeling of sharing and belonging as their reason for joining a gang.

(2) RESPECT- This is something everyone wants and some gang members carry their desire for it to the extreme. Respect is sought for not only the individual, but also for one's set or gang, family, territory, and various other things, real or perceived in the mind of the "gangbanger". Some gangs require, by written or spoken regulation, that the gang member must always show disrespect to rival gang members.

(Referred to in gang slang as 'dis'). If a gang member witnesses a fellow member failing to dis a rival gang through hand signs, graffiti, or a simple "mad dog" or stare-down, they can issue a "violation" to their fellow posse member and he/she can actually be "beaten down" by their own gang as punishment. After the dis has been issued, if it is witnessed, the third "R" will become evident.

(3) RETALIATION / REVENGE- It must be understood that in gang culture, no challenge goes unanswered. Many times, drive-by shootings and other acts of violence follow an event perceived as dis. A common occurrence is a confrontation between a gang set and single rival "gangbanger." Outnumbered, he departs the area and returns with his "homeboys" to complete the confrontation to keep his reputation intact. This may occur immediately or follow a delay for planning and obtaining the necessary equipment to complete the retaliatory strike. It must also be understood that many acts of violence are the result of bad drug deals or infringement on drug territory. Some question the authenticity of gang rivalry in shootings and other acts of violence. However, if a group of individuals are together committing either random or pre-planned violence, aren't they a gang? If the gang aspect is learned about, many crimes can be solved through the use of accurate intelligence gathering techniques by law enforcement agencies dealing with this problem. In gangbanging, today's witness is tomorrow's suspect, is the next day's victim.

GRAFFITI INTERPRETATION

Urban street gang graffiti is the most common way for gangs to communicate their message. Organized graffiti is one of the first signs that street gangs are taking hold in your neighborhood and is also an excellent way to track gang growth, affiliation, and sometimes even provides membership information. Graffiti serves several purposes, all of which is understood by other "gangbangers," even members of rival sets. Graffiti has been called the newspaper or bulletin boards for gangs and communicates many messages, including challenges, warnings, and pronouncements of deeds accomplished or about to occur. Local authorities should establish procedures to deal with this public eyesore. This is an area where the community can band together to show gangs they will not be tolerated. Graffiti should be removed or painted over after it is documented and investigated by the police. Some graffiti is nothing more than "tagging." An example of this is "Johnny loves Mary". Police departments and school officials should be sure someone within their respective departments develops an expertise in reading and understanding graffiti.

Officials should understand that graffiti also develops local flavor, which must be identified. Some examples of street gang graffiti found in central Arkansas are as follows:

This is the six-pointed star, which is the symbol of the Folks. In this example, they have both proudly proclaimed their affiliation and dissed (issued disrespect) to the rival Vice Lords by turning the cane handle upside down (Vice Lords use the upright cane in their graffiti). The Folk Nation pitchfork is upright showing respect. The letters at the six points of the star are symbols of the concepts of the Folk Nation: Life, Loyalty, Love, Wisdom, Knowledge, and Understanding.

This is considered gang "knowledge" and is only a small part of what gang members must learn. In fact, many gang sets have extensive books, usually handwritten, of rules and regulations and gang history. These rules must be memorized. Often, gangs have set meeting dates and read from their "Book", and discuss gang business. In a strange sort of way, these meetings resemble fraternity or civic meetings. Many gang members have told of being "violated" for not knowing certain portions of their knowledge when called upon by a gang leader to recite it.

This is a warning to Blood gang members, rivals of the Folks as well as the Crips. SLOBS is the "put down" word used by Crips and Folks (who appear to be loosely aligning) to describe Blood gang members. Notice that the B is crossed out. This is another "put down" and warning for Bloods to stay away. Serious gang members will always write in a fashion to dis rival gangs. Security should be trained to note these peculiar writings and the individual responsible should be counseled by a person knowledgeable in gang affairs. 187 is part of the California Penal Code number for Homicide and 211 is the same for armed robbery. In many gangs, if members use the word Blood or Crip instead of the dis words, Slob and Crab, a violation can be given.

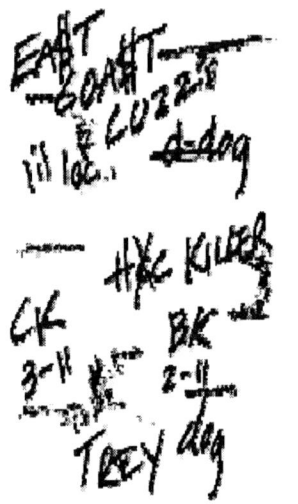

East Coast represents LA gang orientation. "Cuzz" is a term of endearment used by Crips to address each other. Substituting dollar signs for the S's indicates that this gang is selling narcotics.

BK stands for Blood Killer.

Sometimes you will see CK, which of course is Crip Killer.

Street names, signature of artists.

Typical Vice Lord Graffiti--The pyramid and eye of "Allah". The IVL stands for Insane Vice Lords, a Chicago group. CVL or Conservative Vice Lord graffiti is also sometimes seen. The drawing is said to represent the ancient pyramids and their black builders. Note the number of bricks in the pyramid--21. This has significant meaning to a true People Nation member. Note the similarities to some Muslim symbols. Very few if any local gang members have any connection at all to the Muslim faith.

Vice Lord marker and hand sign, sometimes drawn, sometimes used as a hand signal. The Vice Lords and Bloods in the Little Rock area use the five-pointed star.

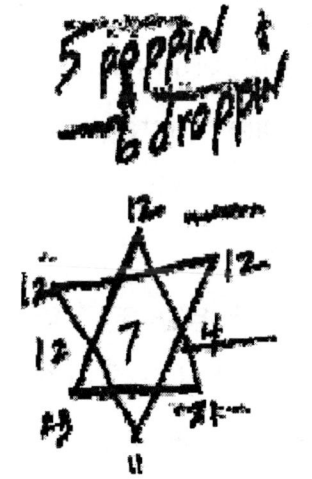

Put down to rival BGD six-pointed star saying the five points of the Vice Lord star is 5 popping (shooting at) the BGD six-pointed star. It should be noted that in some instances, numbers will appear rather than letters in the drawings or graffiti of "bangers". Usually, this is a fairly easy code to break because gangs simply use the number which corresponds to the place the letter falls in the alphabet as in: 2.7.4 = B.G.D. = Black Gangster Disciple 12.12.12 = L.L.L. = Love, Life, Loyalty

Other gangs use other codes and alphabets, which must be deciphered locally. It should be understood that gangs may adopt other types of graffiti or make up their own. That once again illustrates the importance of developing local intelligence about groups by exercising cooperation among law enforcement officials, school authorities, and the general public. Gangs are certainly a community problem, and the community must galvanize to properly respond by dealing with those already involved and offering alternatives to those who accept. While these illustrate gang activity in the Little Rock area, many of the same or similar markings will be found throughout the state and region. Roll call, "RIP", graffiti for a Little Rock Blood gang member killed in a shooting was recently found in a small community three hours away. While many gang members wear certain types of clothing, one must be very careful in assuming that a young person is a "banger" simply because they are wearing a Colorado Rockies or Los Angeles Raiders cap or jacket. Much more evidence is required. Some gang members have said that they joined up because it was trendy and cool while others are intimidated into joining for protection. Other kids who exhibit gang style are, in fact, only "being cool" by dressing the part.

Gang members are not all black. Indeed, one of the largest street gangs in the Little Rock area has only a few black members. Several members of this gang were recently arrested for attempted murder after fire-bombing a home in an attempt at retaliation. We have also identified several all female gangs who have their own reputations that are as ferocious as any of the male gangs. Male gang members privately have even expressed fear of several of the ladies of the female gangs. There are also many white teens who are joining hate groups and various other groups who promote racial disharmony.

These groups appear to be growing in number and may have organized recruitment efforts planned for your area. Recently while speaking to a parent/teacher group, I was told by a mother of her son's activity burning crosses and wearing white robes and hoods. When asked why she allowed this activity, she said she was afraid of her son and would not intervene. Any activity by or information about these groups should be passed along to your local police authorities.

Mara Salvatrucha   MS-13

Mara Salvatrucha is a large gang involved in criminal activities throughout Central and North America. The gang's name is commonly abbreviated as MS-13, Mara, MS, and is composed of mostly of Salvadorians, Hondurans, Mexicans, and Guatemalans. The MS-13 gang has cliques, or factions, located throughout United States, El Salvador, parts of Central America and in some other parts of the world. Membership is believed to total over 100,000 worldwide. MS-13 criminal activities include drug smuggling and sales, black market gun sales, human trafficking, assassinations for hire, theft, and assaults on law enforcement officials. Their activities have caught the eye of the FBI, who in September 2005 initiated wide-scale raids against suspected gang members, netting 650 arrests across the country.

Former gang member Brenda Paz said that MS-13 is well structured, with multiple leaders, and that the gang's goal was to become the top gang in the United States.

History

The gang formed in LA California. Mexican-American gangs would prey on Salvadorian immigrants who came to the U.S. escaping the El Salvador Civil War. The "devil's head" hand signal, which forms an "M" when displayed upside down, bears remarkable resemblance to the same symbol common in hard rock. The founders copied this symbol they saw on their visits to rock concerts. In the beginning the gang was named Mara Salvatrucha Stoners (MSS) when stoner gangs were growing in Los Angeles. The gang only allowed Salvadorans to join but later let other Hispanics join the gang. Many Mara Salvatrucha gang members from the Los Angeles area have been deported either because of their illegal status in the United States, for committing crimes as a non-citizen, or both.

Many have continued their gang activities upon returning to El Salvador. Back in El Salvador, these deportees have recruited more members, including new members who immigrate illegally to the United States.

Infamous crimes

On 2003-07-23 Brenda Paz, a pregnant 18-year old girl was found murdered on the banks of the Shenandoah River in Virginia. Police believed she was killed to prevent her from cooperating in MS-13 related investigations in six states. Four of her friends were later convicted of the murder.

On 2006-05-13, Ernesto "Smokey" Miranda was murdered at his home in El Salvador, a few hours after declining to attend a party for a gang member who had just been released from prison. He had begun studying law and working to keep kids out of gangs.

On 2004-12-23, one of worst MS-13 crimes in Central America happened in Honduras, Chamelecón. An intercity bus was intercepted and sprayed with automatic gunfire, killing some 28 passengers. Those convicted were MS gang-leaders and in February 2007 the courts found Juan Carlos Miralda Bueso and Darwin Alexis Ramírez guilty of several crimes including murder and attempted murder. Ebert Anibal Rivera was another held over the attack and was arrested in Texas after having fled, while another also accused of masterminding the attack, Juan Bautista Jimenez, was killed in prison. According to the authorities his own MS-13 inmates hanged him.

Etymology

There are various possible explanations for the name Mara Salvatrucha. Some sources state the gang is named for La Mara, a street in San Salvador, and the Salvatrucha guerillas that fought in El Salvador's bloody civil war. Additionally, the word 'mara' means gang in Caliche and is taken from marabunta, the name of a fierce type of ant, the word can also imply to the notorious gangs of Maravilla based in the East Los Angeles region. "Salvatrucha" is a portmanteau of Salvadoran and trucha, a Caliche word for being alert, usually entailing preparedness for crime or abuse from police. Mara Salvatrucha is also commonly translated as Salvadoran Gang. Trucha also means trout in Spanish.

Gang markings

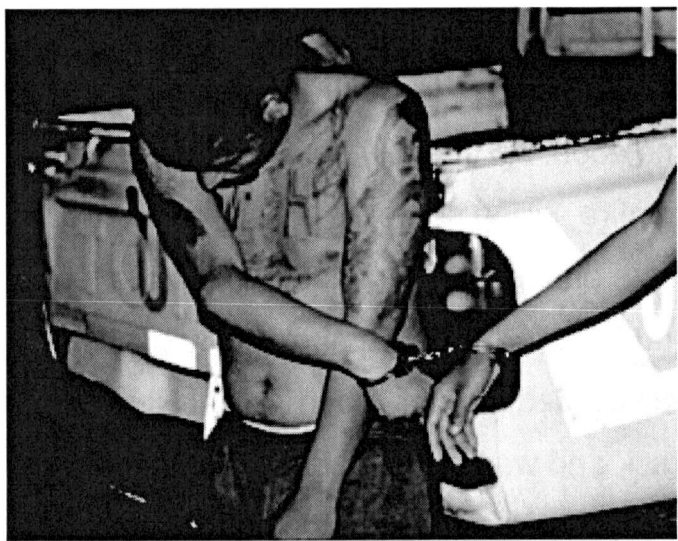

An MS-13 suspect bearing gang tattoos is handcuffed.

In 2004, the FBI created the MS-13 National Gang Task Force. A year later, the FBI helped create National Gang Intelligence Center.

Many Mara Salvatrucha members cover themselves in tattoos. Common markings include:

- **MS-13**
- **MS**
- **13**
- **18**
- **"Salvadorian Pride"**
- **The "Devil Horns" and the name of their Clique.**

Outlaw Biker Gangs in Canada

Born in Canada, this author has personal experience when it comes to riding a 'Patch' and living in the world of Outlaw bikers. As the old saying goes *'you can pick your friends…but you can't pick your family!'* Riding with an OMG, is a dangerous existence in a world that does not suffer fools. The following passage is a tribulation to this fact:

Petra Smith*, a 36-year-old mother of three, spent nearly 15 years as the "ol' lady" of a Canadian OMG member. Free of them now for two years, she is under the RCMP police protection program. She says fiercely: "I want girls who think one-percenters are cool to understand what they're getting into." "The first time I ever went to their clubhouse, some hangaround got out of line. The boys dragged him downstairs to the basement, six or eight of them, and beat him with baseball bats for at least half an hour. Then they threw him out back, all bloody, to the Rottweilers." She doesn't know if the victim survived. On a later occasion the gang rented the penthouse suite of a U.S. hotel. They lured up a "citizen" -- their name for people like you and me -- got him drunk, then put a pillow over his face and shot him in the head. Petra and another mamma had to clean up the blood and brains.

* *Her real name is not given to protect her identity.*

Roadhouse Doc Holiday and his 77 Shovelhead called "The Crow"

According to the Outlaws Motorcycle Club, law-enforcement officials changed the meaning of " 1%er " in the 1980s so that the term referred to members of criminal gangs. The Outlaws says it is a law-abiding organization whose members share a commitment to biking and brotherhood. According to Criminal Intelligence Service Canada, the Hells Angels is the foremost organized crime group in the country, topping traditional Mafia and ethnic gangs. The Hells Angels began in 1948 in California and has grown to a network of 1800 members in 22 countries. It's estimated that Canada has about 500 full-fledged members in 32 active chapters across the country. The largest and most-feared chapter of the Hells Angels was formed in Montreal. In 1977, it merged with another gang called the Popeye.

The FBI estimates the Hells Angels takes in $1 billion a year worldwide from drug trafficking. In Quebec, the Rock Machine emerged in 1986 and quickly became the biggest rival of the Hells Angels. A turf war between the two gangs in the late 1990s claimed 150 lives, including two prison guards and 11-year-old Daniel Desrochers, who died when a car bomb exploded outside a biker hangout. His death and the outrage that followed prompted Bill C-95, the legislation that stiffens penalties for convicted offenders who are shown to be members of established criminal organizations. According to the CISC's 2004 report, the anti-gang law seems to be having an impact. The agency says the law has persuaded two of Canada's major bike gangs - the Outlaws and the Bandidos - to keep a low profile. The report added that of seven Outlaws chapters in Canada, only three were operating with any kind of stability. Even the Hells Angels, the report said, were "experiencing varying degrees of weakness in Alberta, Manitoba, Quebec and Atlantic Canada due to law-enforcement operations, internal conflict and increased competition from other criminal organizations."

According to police, biker gangs share several characteristics:

- They show off their colors in public.

- Biker gangs use force and violence to survive and grow.

- Intimidation, arms and explosives are their weapons of choice.

- The organizations have a hierarchical structure.

- Committing crimes is left to new recruits while those higher up reap the rewards.

- The hierarchical structure allows the leaders to operate with impunity while flaunting their image of power to attract recruits and draw them into crime.

It is difficult for law-enforcement agencies to infiltrate these organizations because becoming a member often involves committing murder. North American clubs also tend to require their members to own American-made bikes, often Harley-Davidsons.

Here's a brief look at the major biker organizations that have operated in Canada.

Hells Angels

Criminal Intelligence Service Canada describes the Hells Angels as the largest "outlaw motorcycle gang" in the country, with at least 32 active chapters and 500 members, especially in Quebec, Ontario and British Columbia. In its 2004 report, CISC said the Angels derive "significant financial income from various criminal activities across the country such as prostitution, fraud and extortion. However, drug trafficking, particularly cocaine, marijuana and increasingly methamphetamine, remains the primary source of illicit income." The gang moved into Ontario in 2000. Before that, its only presence in the province was with a chapter of the Nomads, the club's elite branch. The Nomads don't tie themselves to geographical locations and don't have formal clubhouses, like other chapters. Within a year, the Angels had absorbed members of the Para Dice Riders, Satan's Choice and Last Chance, giving them at least 100 members in the Toronto area - the highest concentration of Hells Angels in the world. In April 2007, police raided 40 Hells Angels locations in three provinces and arrested more than 30 people. Included in the raids was the largest clubhouse in Canada, the Hells Angels' downtown Toronto building.

Bandidos

The Bandidos were founded in the 1960s in Texas. The club's old guard was said to be against its absorption of the Rock Machine's Ontario branches for fear of igniting the same kind of war with the Hells Angels that gripped Quebec for much of the 1990s and left at least 150 people dead. The Bandidos have established a strong presence in Ontario and recently set up a "probationary" chapter in Winnipeg. In April 2006, eight people were found dead in a farmer's field near the small town of Shedden, Ont., about 30 kilometers southwest of London. Police said the killings virtually wiped out the Toronto chapter of the Bandidos.

Outlaws

The world's second most powerful criminal biker gang - although it trails far behind the Hells Angels in Canada. First established in the United States in 1935. The gang came to Canada in 1978 when several chapters of Satan's Choice in Montreal changed allegiance and set up shop as the Outlaws Motorcycle Club of Canada. The group is known to detest members of the Hells Angels.

Rock Machine

Second only to Hells Angels in Quebec. A long-running turf war with the Angels left more than 150 people dead as the two fought over the lucrative trade in illegal drugs. The war also led to the passage of anti-gang legislation by the federal government.

As the Hells Angels expanded into Ontario, so did the Rock Machine. The organization established three chapters. In 2001, it aligned itself with the Texas-based Bandidos.

Satan's Choice

Once one of Ontario's strongest motorcycle gangs, Satan's Choice became part of the Hells Angels' 2000-2001 expansion into Ontario. Satan's Choice had branches in Keswick, Kitchener, Oshawa, Sudbury, Simcoe County, Thunder Bay and Toronto - but nothing outside the province.

Para Dice Riders

Once considered Ontario's strongest biker gang, its membership was limited to the Toronto area. The group was absorbed by the Hells Angels in 2001, when the Angels moved into Ontario.

Last Chance

Another small Ontario-based biker gang that agreed to switch over to the Hells Angels when the world's most power biker gang moved into the province.

Lobos

Originally concentrated in the Windsor, Ont., area, the Lobos motorcycle gang decided to take up the Hells Angels on its offer of merger in 2001.

Loners

The Loners Motorcycle Club was founded in Ontario in 1979 with a handful of chapters, including a now-defunct one in southwestern Ontario that was headed by Wayne Kellestine. As part of its Ontario expansion drive, the Hells Angels tried to persuade the St. Thomas Loners chapter to join the Angels. Kellestine - who was injured in an assassination attempt in 1999 -resisted. The club has expanded to the United States and Europe, but in Ontario, its highest profile in recent years was a legal fight by a Toronto chapter to keep its mascot on its property north of the city, in 2001. The neutered, declawed lion named Woody was moved to an animal sanctuary.

Vagabonds

Another Ontario-based motorcycle gang that was more or less absorbed by the Hells Angels when it expanded into Ontario in 2000-2001.

The Red Devils

Said to be the oldest motorcycle gang in Canada. The group is made up of a couple of dozen members concentrated in the Hamilton, Ont. area.

Overview

Traditional rules for participation in a Motorcycle Club, including, but not limited to, a group of elected officers; a probationary period for new members; the wearing of a specific club patch (or patches) adorned with the term "MC"; a measure of privacy about their internal structure, bylaws, and membership; and some level of sworn allegiance to other members of the club. The typical internal organization of a motorcycle club consists of a president, vice president, treasurer, secretary, road captain, and sergeant-at-arms. Localized groups of a single, large MC are called chapters, and the first chapter established for an MC is referred to as the mother chapter. The president of the mother chapter serves as the president of the entire MC, and sets club policy on a variety of issues.

There are a great many clubs for motorcycle riders who refer to themselves generically as motorcycle clubs. Though they are grammatically correct, these clubs are not MCs in the strictest sense of the term, and members of MCs (as defined in this article) regard these other clubs as motorcycle riding clubs. MC members are not usually referred to by their given names, but instead refer to each other by nicknames, or road names, sometimes even displaying their road name on the club vest. Whether or not this practice was carried over from the military aviation history of colorful pilot call signs is not known.

History

The earliest motorcycle clubs were started following World War II by pilots looking for the same thrills they experienced during the war, though the reputed oldest motorcycle club is the Yonkers MC, founded in 1903. Other notable early clubs include the San Francisco MC.

Membership

The membership process for most motorcycle clubs begins as a guest or "hang-around", wherein an individual is invited to some club events or meets club members at known gathering places. If the guest is interested, they may ask to become a member. If accepted, they remain a prospective member, or prospect, for some minimum time period, participating in some club activities, but not having voting privileges, while they are evaluated for suitability as full members. Some clubs refer to a potential member as a probationary member or probate. Though probationary status is usually reserved for those that already have the necessary knowledge and experience to be members. For example, if an entire chapter switches from one club to another, the members are Probationary members for some period of time. Some amount of hazing may occur during the prospecting period, ranging from the mandatory performance of menial labor tasks for full patch members to sophomoric pranks, and, in the case of some outlaw motorcycle clubs, acts of civil disobedience or crime. During this time, the prospect may wear the club name on the back of their vest, but not the full logo, though this practice may vary from club to club.

To become a full member, the prospect or probate must be voted on by the rest of the full club members. Successful admission usually requires more than a simple majority, and some clubs may reject a prospect or a probate for a single dissenting vote. Some form of formal induction follows, where in the new member affirms his loyalty to the club and its members. The final logo ' Center' patch is then awarded. Full members are often referred to as "full patch members" or "full patch holders" and the step of attaining full membership can be referred to as "being patched".

One-percent MCs do not allow women to become members.

Colors

The primary visual identification of a member of an MC is the vest adorned with a specific large club patch or patches, predominantly located in the middle of the back. The 'Center Patch' will contain a club logo. The name of the club will be on the top patch which is called a 'Rocker'., and the bottom rocker will contain the name of a possible state, province, or country. Sometimes the bottom rocker says 'Nomad' this means the member has no home base and moves around from chapter to chapter. The vest and the patches themselves are referred to as the "colors". The colors for some clubs can consist of a single, one-piece patch, while other clubs may have a three (or more) piece patch. The club patches always remain property of the club itself, not the member, and only members are allowed to wear the clubs colors. A member must closely guard their colors. Allowing one's colors to fall into the hands of an outsider is an act of disgrace and may result in loss of membership in a club, or worse. One MC successfully sued a law enforcement agency for the return of a members colors following a police raid.

Outlaw Biker Gangs in the USA

*This author would like to thank Brother David Ball for his assistance with the following information.

Motorcycle clubs are often perceived as criminal organizations or, at best, gangs of hoodlums or thugs by traditional society. This perception has been fueled by the movies, popular culture, and highly publicized isolated incidents, the earliest of which was a brawl in Hollister, California in 1947 between members of the Boozefighters MC (motto: a drinking club with a motorcycle problem) and the Pissed Off Bastards MC (precursor to the Hells Angels). The press asked the American Motorcyclist Association (AMA) to comment, and their response was that 99% of motorcyclists were law-abiding citizens, and the last one percent were outlaws. Thus was born the term, "one percenter" – " 1%er". During the 1940's and 1950's, at rallies and gatherings sponsored by the AMA, prizes were awarded for nicest club uniform, prettiest motorcycle, and so forth. Some clubs, however, rejected the clean-cut image and adopted the "one percenter" mark, even going so far as to create a diamond (rhombus) shaped patch labeled "1%" to wear on their vests as a badge of honor. The 1% patch is also used to instill fear and respect from the general public and other motorcyclists. Other clubs wore (and still wear) upside down AMA patches. Another practice was to cut their one piece club patches into three or more pieces as a form of protest, which evolved into the current form of three piece colors worn by many MCs today.

One percent clubs point out that the term simply means that they are simply committed to "Riding and Brotherhood", where riding isn't a weekend activity, but a way of life. These clubs assert that local and national law enforcement agencies have co-opted the term to paint them as criminals. While it is a fact that individual members of some MCs, and even entire chapters have engaged in felonious behavior, other members and supporters of these clubs insist that these are isolated occurrences and that the clubs, as a whole, are not criminal organizations. They often compare themselves to police departments, wherein the occasional "bad cop" does not make a police department a criminal organization, either. At least one biker website has a news section devoted to "cops gone bad" to support their point of view. Many one percenter clubs, including the Hells Angels, sponsor charitable events throughout the year for such causes as Salvation Army shelters and Toys for Tots. Alternatively, both the Federal Bureau of Investigation (FBI) and Criminal Intelligence Service Canada (CISC) have designated certain MCs as Outlaw Motorcycle Gangs (OMGs), among them the Pagans, Hells Angels, Outlaws MC, and Bandidos. Canada, especially, has experienced a significant upsurge in crime involving members and associates of these MCs, most notably in what has been dubbed the Quebec Biker war. Some members of the Hells Angels MC have been indicted on various charges, including RICO charges, murder, robbery, extortion, trafficking in stolen and VIN-switched motorcycles, methamphetamine and cocaine distribution. As recently as September 29, 2006, the president and another officer of the San Francisco chapter of the Hells Angels were indicted on charges of methamphetamine and cocaine distribution.

Relationships between MCs

In the United States, most MCs have established statewide MC confederations. These confederations are usually composed of most MCs who have chapters in the state, and the occasional interested third party organization. The confederation holds periodic meetings on neutral ground, wherein representatives from each club (usually the presidents and vice-presidents, but not always) meet in closed session to resolve disputes between clubs and discuss issues of common interest. The largest one-percent club tends to dominate the confederation, using their numbers to force their will on the other clubs. Sometimes clubs are forced into "support" roles for a one-percent club. Smaller clubs who resist a large one-percent club have been forcibly disbanded and stripped of their colors.

Smaller clubs usually comply, since members of a family club are usually unwilling to risk injury or worse. Some large one-percent MCs are rivals with each other and will fight over territory and other issues. In 2002, members of the Mongols MC and the Hells Angels MC had a confrontation in Laughlin, Nevada at the Harrah's Laughlin Casino that left three bikers dead. Police intelligence reports indicate that the Mongols initiated the confrontation to bolster their status. Another melee between the Hells Angels and the Pagans MC occurred in February 2002 at a Hells Angels convention. Police reports indicate the Pagans were outraged that the event was held on what the Pagans considered their "home turf".

Notable United States Motorcycle Gangs

- Hells Angels MC

- Mongols MC

- Pagans MC

- Bandidos MC

- Outlaws MC

- Boozefighters MC

- Yonkers MC - the oldest MC in the United States

- San Francisco MC -the second oldest MC in the United States

Ivan 'Doc' Holiday & Brother David Ball

Racially Motivated Gangs

Aryan Brotherhood (AB)

Gender Makeup: Male

Racial Makeup: White

Origin: Originated in 1967 in the San Quentin State Prison, California Department of Corrections.

Characteristics:

Unaffiliated splinter groups sometimes use the name of their state along with the name "Aryan Brotherhood" (e.g., Aryan Brotherhood of Texas). Members display many white supremacist, neo-nazi characteristics and ideology, but often state their goals as simply "getting high and getting over," or making their stay in the prison as comfortable as possible. Members are ordinarily apolitical. Most are in custody for crimes such as robbery.

- Identifiers/Symbols/Tattoos:
- Shamrock cloverleaf
- Initials "AB"
- Swastikas
- Double lighting bolts
- The numbers "666"
- Known to use Gaelic (old Irish) symbols as a method of coding communications

Aryan Brotherhood groups from other states often accompany the symbols mentioned above with the name of the state.

Enemies/Rivals:

The AB maintains a working relationship with the Mexican Mafia (EME) and therefore opposes the EME's long-time enemy, the La Nuestra Familia (NF). The Aryan Brotherhood has traditionally nurtured a deep hatred toward black individuals and members of black groups/gangs, such as the:

- Black Guerrilla Family (BGF)
- Crips
- Bloods
- El Rukns

Allies:

Maintains a working relationship with the Mexican Mafia (EME).

Is known to give moral support to black groups in an effort to encourage possible prison disturbances.

Utilizes black associates to buy and sell drugs to elements of the black prison population.

Compatibles with most motorcycle gangs; many members were former "1 % Bikers."

Compatible with most white supremacy groups. This often leads to confusion in distinguishing AB members from other white supremacist groups, particularly when making identification by their tattoos or symbols.

True members generally tolerate "Copy cat" Aryan Brotherhood groups. However, federal and California AB's do not consider them to be legitimate and may threaten violence if AB tattoos are not burned or cut off.

They actively cooperates with the Dirty White Boys, an Anglo spin-off gang of the Texas Syndicate. Similar cooperation has been observed with the Silent Brotherhood.

Recruitment/Initiation:

- Membership in the AB has traditionally come from white male inmates.
- Lifelong allegiance is a requirement.
- A "Blood in, blood out" oath must be taken.
- Often a "hit" or significant act of violence is required before full membership is earned.
- Candidacy for membership may last a year or more.

Propensity for Disruptive Behavior:

Aryan Brotherhood is not readily recognizable; however, receipt of inmates on interstate compact and the current membership in groups with white supremacy ideology lend to the threat of an organizing AB within our facilities. Main activities of the AB are centered on drug trafficking, extortion, pressure rackets, and internal discipline.

Prison activities include introduction of contraband, distribution of drugs, and getting past facility rules and regulations.

Traditionally, targets have been non-gang inmates and internal discipline.

From 1975 to 1985, members committed 40 homicides in California prisons and local jails, as well as 13 homicides in the community.

From 1978 to 1992, AB members, suspects, and associates in the federal system were involved in 26 homicides, 3 of which involved staff victims.

Once released from custody, AB members are actively expected to continue to assist or "score" for the members remaining in prison.

International Organized Crime

When you think of organized crime, you probably picture the Italian and Sicilian Mafioso of television and the silver screen. But in recent years, the face of organized crime has changed, and the threat is broader and more complex than ever. Today, organized crime includes:

Russian mobsters who fled to the U.S. in the wake of the Soviet Union's collapse; Groups from African countries like Nigeria that engage in drug trafficking and financial scams, Chinese tongs, Japanese Yakusa, and other Asian crime rings as well as Enterprises based in Eastern European nations like Hungary and Romania. All of these groups have a presence in the U.S. or are targeting our citizens from afar—using the Internet and other technologies of our global age. More and more, they are literally becoming partners in crime, realizing they have more to gain from cooperating than competing.

The Impact of Organized Crime

It isn't easily measured, but we know it's significant. Organized crime rings manipulate and monopolize financial markets, traditional institutions like labor unions, and legitimate industries like construction and trash hauling. They bring drugs into our cities and raise the level of violence in our communities by buying off corrupt officials and using graft, extortion, intimidation, and murder to maintain their operations. Their underground businesses—including prostitution and human trafficking—sew misery nationally and globally. They also con us out of millions each year through various stock frauds and financial scams. The economic impact alone is staggering: it's estimated that global organized crime reaps illegal profits of around $1 trillion per year.

Italian Mafia

Since their appearance in the 1800s, the Italian criminal societies known as the Mafia have infiltrated the social and economic fabric of Italy and now impact the world. They are some of the most notorious and widespread of all criminal societies.

 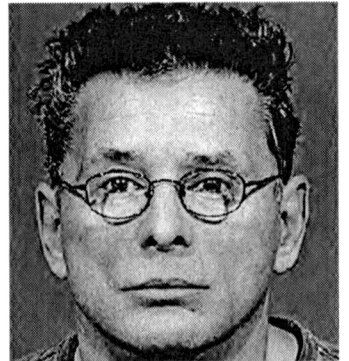

John Gotti (The Teflon Don) & Sammy 'The Bull' Gravano

There are several groups currently active in the U.S.; the Sicilian Mafia; the Camorra or Neapolitan Mafia; the 'Ndrangheta or Calabrian Mafia; and the Sacra Corona Unita or United Sacred Crown. We estimate the four groups have approximately 25,000 members total, with 250,000 affiliates worldwide. There are more than 3,000 members and affiliates in the U.S., scattered mostly throughout the major cities in the Northeast, the Midwest, California, and the South. Their largest presence centers around New York, southern New Jersey, and Philadelphia. Their criminal activities are international with members and affiliates in Canada, South America, Australia, and parts of Europe. They are also known to collaborate with other international organized crime groups from all over the world, especially in drug trafficking. The major threats to American society posed by these groups are drug trafficking and money laundering.

They have been involved in heroin trafficking for decades. Two major investigations that targeted Italian organized crime drug trafficking in the 1980s are known as the "French Connection" and the "Pizza Connection." These groups don't limit themselves to drug running. They're also involved in illegal gambling, political corruption, extortion, kidnapping, fraud, counterfeiting, infiltration of legitimate businesses, murders, bombings, and weapons trafficking. Industry experts in Italy estimate that their worldwide criminal activity is worth more than $100 billion annually.

History

These enterprises evolved over the course of 3,000 years during numerous periods of invasion and exploitation by numerous conquering armies in Italy. Over the millennia, Sicilians became more clannish and began to rely on familial ties for safety, protection, justice, and survival. An underground secret society formed initially as resistance fighters against the invaders and to exact frontier vigilante justice against oppression. A member was known as a "Man Of Honor," respected and admired because he protected his family and friends and kept silent even unto death. Sicilians weren't concerned if the group profited from its actions because it came at the expense of the oppressive authorities. These secret societies eventually grew into the Mafia. Since the 1900s, thousands of Italian organized crime figures—mostly Sicilian Mafiosi—have come illegally to the US. Many who fled here in the early 1920s helped establish what is known today as La Cosa Nostra or the American Mafia. Charles "Lucky" Luciano, a Mafioso from Sicily, came to the U.S. during this era and is credited for making the American La Cosa Nostra what it is today. Luciano structured the La Cosa Nostra after the Sicilian Mafia. When Luciano was deported back to Italy in 1946 for operating a prostitution ring, he became a liaison between the Sicilian Mafia and La Cosa Nostra.

La Cosa Nostra

La Cosa Nostra is the foremost organized criminal threat to American society. Literally translated into English it means "this thing of ours." It is a nationwide alliance of criminals—linked by blood ties or through conspiracy—dedicated to pursuing crime and protecting its members. La Cosa Nostra, or the LCN as it is known by the FBI, consists of different "families" or groups that are generally arranged geographically and engaged in significant and organized racketeering activity. It is also known as the Mafia, a term used to describe other organized crime groups.

The LCN is most active in the New York metropolitan area, parts of New Jersey, Philadelphia, Detroit, Chicago, and New England. It has members in other major cities and is involved in international crimes.

History of La Cosa Nostra

Although La Cosa Nostra has its roots in Italian organized crime; it has been a separate organization for many years. Today, La Cosa Nostra cooperates in various criminal activities with different criminal groups that are headquartered in Italy. Giuseppe Esposito was the first known Sicilian Mafia member to emigrate to the U.S. He and six other Sicilians fled to New York after murdering the chancellor and a vice chancellor of a Sicilian province and 11 wealthy landowners. He was arrested in New Orleans in 1881 and extradited to Italy. New Orleans was also the site of the first major Mafia incident in this country. On October 15, 1890, New Orleans Police Superintendent David Hennessey was murdered execution-style. Hundreds of Sicilians were arrested, and 19 were eventually indicted for the murder. An acquittal generated rumors of widespread bribery and intimidated witnesses.

Outraged citizens of New Orleans organized a lynch mob and killed 11 of the 19 defendants. Two were hanged, nine were shot, and the remaining eight escaped. The American Mafia has evolved over the years as various gangs assumed—and lost—dominance over the years: the Black Hand gangs around 1900; the Five Points Gang in the 1910s and '20s in New York City; Al Capone's Syndicate in Chicago in the 1920s. By the end of the '20s, two primary factions had emerged, leading to a war for control of organized crime in New York City. The murder of faction leader Joseph Masseria brought an end to the gang warfare, and the two groups united to form the organization now dubbed La Cosa Nostra. It was not a peaceful beginning: Salvatore

Maranzano, the first leader of La Cosa Nostra, was murdered within six months. Charles "Lucky" Luciano became the new leader. Maranzano had established the La Cosa Nostra code of conduct, set up the

Charles "Lucky" Luciano

"family" divisions and structure, and established procedures for resolving disputes. Luciano set up the "Commission" to rule all La Cosa Nostra activities. The Commission included bosses from six or seven families. Luciano was deported back to Italy in 1946 based on his conviction for operating a prostitution ring. There, he became a liaison between the Sicilian Mafia and La Cosa Nostra.

Russian Criminal Enterprises

The Russian Mob or Mafia, Russkaya Mafiya, Red Mafia, Krasnaya Mafiya or Bratva (brotherhood), is a name given to a broad group of organized criminals of various ethnicity, which appeared in the former Soviet Union territories after its disintegration in 1991.

History

Despite seeming to arise during the Fall of the Soviet Union, organized crime had existed throughout the imperial and communist eras as a form of open rebellion against the systems in the form of the "Thief's World". During this time organized crime was fiercely honor-based and often attacked and killed traitors among their ranks. Nevertheless, during World War II, many enlisted in the Russian Army resulting in the Suka Wars, which killed many of the thieves who were branded as government allies as well as the original thief underworld during Stalin's reign.

The criminals, seeking a new survival strategy, began to ally with the elite in the Soviet Union as a means of survival, creating a powerful Russian black market. The real breakthrough for criminal organizations occurred during the economic disaster and mass immigration of the 1990s that followed the fall of the Soviet Union. Desperate for money, many former government workers turned to crime, others joined the large numbers of Soviet citizens who moved overseas primarily to the United States and the Mafia became a natural extension of this trend. According to official estimates, some 100,000 Russians are committed mobsters, with a large but unknown number engaging in these criminal practices on and off.

Backed by its extensive connection to the apparatchick power network of the Soviet Union, between 1992 and 1994 the Russian Mafia targeted the commercial centers of power, seizing control of the nation's fragile banking system. At first the criminal gangs were content to merely "park" their large cash holdings in legitimate institutions, but soon they realized that the next step was the easiest of all: direct ownership of the bank itself.

Banking executives, reform-minded business leaders, even investigative journalists, were systematically assassinated or kidnapped. In 1993 alone, members of the eight criminal gangs that control the Moscow underworld murdered 10 local bankers. Calling themselves "Thieves in Law" (vori v zakone), Russian gangsters have murdered ninety-five bankers in the last five years. Beginning in the late 1970s systematically, the Communist bloc began encouraging large numbers of its people to emigrate to the United States and Europe. Encouraged by diplomatic feelers put out by the Soviet government, both the Carter and Reagan Administration in association with the government of Israel, began pushing for the emigration of the Soviets large Jewish population. That was soon joined by other non-Jewish ethnicities. By the late 1980s large colonies of former Soviet and Communist bloc subjects had been established throughout the United States. Most of these ethnic colonies became dominated by the Soviet crime groups who answered to their associates and superiors in the USSR. After the fall of the Soviet Union that emigration increased. Via their large communities throughout the West and in particular the United States, since the mid-90s the crime groups have been trying to expand their criminal empire into America, most often via the trafficking of drugs and illegal weapons. This has led to some brutal wars with the organizations already present, including the Italian Mafia, Chinese Triads, Irish Mob the Latino Narcos, Mexican Gangs and the Japanese Yakuza all of whom also had their own communities to operate inside of with protection.

This has led to a number of alliances between the gangs of the former USSR and others. The group is believed to have links to Colombian drug smugglers and many smaller gangs as a result of the fall of the Soviet Union. Some also believe they are at the heart of gangs smuggling illegal workers west to the European Union and often Britain, though no proof has been offered for this at this time. The home of the Russian Mafia in America is in the Brighton Beach (dubbed by Russians "Little Odessa") neighborhood in Brooklyn, New York City. Over the last few years, the FBI and Russian security services have tried to crack down on the Mafia, though the impact of this has yet to be measured. Amid the political uncertainty that has engulfed the former Soviet Union since the end of the Cold War in 1991; rampant, unchecked organized crime has laid waste to noteworthy democratic reforms and contributed to an economic and moral meltdown within the 15 newly independent republics. Intelligence reports emanating out of Russia peg the numerical size of the Russian Mafia ("mafiya") at 100,000 members owing allegiance to 8,000 stratified crime groups who control 70-80% of all private business and 40% of the nation's wealth. Many of the bosses and main members of the Russian mafia are believed to be ex-Soviet Army and ex-KGB officers who lost their posts in the reduction of forces that began in 1993 after the end of the Cold War. It is also believed that many of the groups' enforcers are ex-Russian Spetsnaz Special Forces, an organization renowned for its brutality.

Russian mobsters also recruit sportsmen: boxers, martial artists, weightlifters (as funding for sports had decreased sharply) and other Olympic athletes. In some cases, the Russian mafia has recruited Olympic sharpshooters to carry out hits. The Russian Mafia appears to be organized in similar ways to the Italian mafia. It is believed, however, to be a very loose organization with internal feuds and murders being commonplace. A particularly brutal practice rumored to be utilized by the Russian Mafia is the killing of not only the individual who has "snitched" or turned against the Organizatsiya, but also the individual's family. The Russian mafia is notorious for underground operations and clean transactions, and, unlike certain vestiges of the Italian mafia, it is known for its secrecy and unflamboyant manner.

Asian Criminal Enterprises

Asian criminal enterprises have been operating in the U.S. since the early 1900s. The first of these groups evolved from Chinese tongs— social organizations formed by early Chinese-American immigrants. A century later, the criminalized tongs are thriving and have been joined by similar organizations with ties to East and Southeast Asia. Members of the most dominant Asian criminal enterprises affecting the U.S. have ties—either directly or culturally—to China, Korea, Japan, Thailand, the Philippines, Cambodia, Laos, and Vietnam. Other enterprises are emerging as threats, however, including groups from the South Pacific island nations. These enterprises rely on extensive networks of national and international criminal associates that are fluid and extremely mobile.

They adapt easily to the changes around them, have multilingual abilities, can be highly sophisticated in their criminal operations, and have extensive financial capabilities. Some enterprises have commercialized their criminal activities and can be considered business firms of various sizes, from small family-run operations to large corporations. Asian criminal enterprises have prospered thanks largely to the globalization of the world economies and to communications technology and international travel. Generous immigration policies have provided many members of Asian criminal enterprises the ability to enter and live on every populated continent in the world today undetected. There are two categories of Asian criminal enterprises. Traditional criminal enterprises include the Chinese triads (or underground societies) based in Hong Kong, Taiwan, and Macau as well as the Japanese Yakuza or Boryokudan. Non-traditional criminal enterprises include groups such as Chinese criminally influenced tongs, triad affiliates, and other ethnic Asian street gangs found in several countries with sizeable Asian communities. Asian criminal enterprises conduct traditional racketeering activities normally associated with organized crime: extortion, murder, kidnapping, illegal gambling, prostitution, and loan sharking. They also smuggle aliens, traffic heroin and methamphetamine; commit financial frauds; steal autos and computer chips; counterfeit computer and clothing products; and launder money. There are several trends among Asian criminal enterprises. First, it is more common to see criminal groups cooperate across ethnic and racial heritage lines. Also, some gangs and criminal enterprises have begun to structure their groups in a hierarchical fashion to be more competitive, and the criminal activities they engage in have become globalized.

Finally, more of these criminal enterprises are engaging in white-collar crimes and are co-mingling their illegal activities with legitimate business ventures. In the U.S., Asian criminal enterprises have been identified in more than 50 metropolitan areas. They are more prevalent in Boston, Chicago, Honolulu, Las Vegas, Los Angeles, New Orleans, New York, Newark, Philadelphia, Portland, San Francisco, Seattle, and Washington, D.C.

African Criminal Enterprises

African criminal enterprises have developed quickly since the 1980s due to the globalization of the world's economies and the great advances in communications technology. Easier international travel, expanded world trade, and financial transactions that cross national borders have enabled them to branch out of local and regional crime to target international victims and develop criminal networks within more prosperous countries and regions. The political, social, and economic conditions in African countries like Nigeria, Ghana, and Liberia also have helped some enterprises expand globally. African criminal enterprises have been identified in several major metropolitan areas in the U.S., but are most prevalent in Atlanta, Baltimore, Chicago, Dallas, Houston, Milwaukee, Newark, New York, and Washington, D.C. Nigerian criminal enterprises are the most significant of these groups and operate in more than 80 other countries of the world. They are among the most aggressive and expansionist international criminal groups and are primarily engaged in drug trafficking and financial frauds. The most profitable activity of the Nigerian groups is drug trafficking: delivering heroin from Southeast and Southwest Asia into Europe and the U.S. and cocaine from South America into Europe and South Africa. Large populations of ethnic Nigerians in India, Pakistan, and Thailand have given these enterprises direct access to 90 percent of the world's heroin production. The associated money laundering has helped establish Nigerian criminal enterprises on every populated continent of the world. Nigerian groups are famous globally for their financial frauds, which cost the U.S. alone an estimated $1 billion to $2 billion each year. Schemes are diverse, targeting individuals, businesses, and government offices.

Here's just a partial list of their fraudulent activities: insurance fraud involving auto accidents; healthcare billing scams; life insurance schemes; bank, check, and credit card fraud; advance-fee schemes known as 4-1-9 letters; and document fraud to develop false identities. The advent of the Internet and e-mail has made their crimes more profitable and prevalent.

Dealing with Organized Crime members in your nightclub or bar.

Of this the author is no doubt an expert in the field.

- Be aware of OC members in your club or involved with the club.
- Identify the number of OC members present.
- Identify the type of OC members (Street gang, Outlaw biker etc..)
- Identify hierarchy (the chain of command)
- Identify OC related markings and signs. (Colors and tattoos etc..)
- Make field notes of vehicles, colors, tattoos, activity etc…
- Inform all security personnel of the OC members in the club.
- Security should use the deception that they are unaware of the OC members being in the club/bar.
- It's the cooler's job to work the OC area and to do it single-handedly. Too many security members will just draw unwanted attention and possible confrontation.
- Keep all patrons away from the area that the OC are occupying.
- At the sign of any trouble 'Call the Police Immediately!!'
- If they try to recruit you, tell them you have family in law enforcement and avoid personal contact as much as possible.
- Stay professional in all manners of contact. Do not try to befriend these individuals – Stay neutral at all times.

OC and security interaction and negotiations

- Always speak to the highest-ranking OC member if possible.

- Never show up in force to speak to OC members. Let the cooler do the talking and keep security on alert but far back. This shows the OC members that there is no one challenging them.

- Have a secret hand signal that will have the police called immediately should any kind of trouble start.

- Never come across as being a tough guy or they will call you on it.

- Never 'Order' always 'Ask'.

- Never 'Advise' always 'Explain'

- Never 'Stare' always 'Just a momentary look'.

- RESPECT is crucial!! Show respect but be committed to your duty.

- Never grab an OC member if a fight breaks out, <u>grab the patron</u> and get them out of harms way.

- Never take or allow anyone to take pictures of OC members, their material possessions or their women.

- Watch the associates, probates and prospects, remember the non-members trying to get into the OC gang can be more dangerous than the members.

- If you feel the OC members are flexing a little too much muscle, call and have the local police visit for a cup of coffee. (This is where it's good to have friends in local law enforcement).

- If removing gang symbols off the establishment walls outside, be sure it is done early in the morning and as a group never just one or two persons. No one wants to be singled out by gang members.

- <u>Never divulge any personal information about yourself, your co-workers or the business to any person connected to OC.</u>

TERRORISM

Introduction

From 1983 to 1991, the Federal Bureau of Investigation identified 101 terrorist incidents in the United States. Most terrorist incidents in the United States have been bombing attacks, involving detonated and un-detonated explosive devices, tear gas, pipe bombs and fire bombs. The effects of terrorism can vary significantly from loss of life and injuries to property damage and disruptions in services such as electricity, water supply, public transportation and communications.

One way governments attempt to reduce our vulnerability to terrorist incidents is by increasing security at airports and other public facilities. The U.S. government also works with other countries to limit the sources of support for terrorism.

WHAT IS TERRORISM?

Terrorism is the use of force or violence against persons or property in violation of the criminal laws of the United States for purposes of intimidation, coercion or ransom. Terrorists often use threats to create fear among the public, to try to convince citizens that their government is powerless to prevent terrorism, and to get immediate publicity for their causes. The Federal Bureau of Investigation (FBI) categorizes terrorism in the United States as one of two types--domestic terrorism or international terrorism.

Domestic terrorism involves groups or individuals whose terrorist activities are directed at elements of our government or population without foreign direction. International terrorism involves groups or individuals whose terrorist activities are foreign-based and/or directed by countries or groups outside the United States or whose activities transcend national boundaries.

BIOLOGICAL AND CHEMICAL WEAPONS

Biological agents are infectious microbes or toxins used to produce illness or death in people, animals or plants. Biological agents can be dispersed as aerosols or airborne particles. Terrorists may use biological agents to contaminate food or water because they are extremely difficult to detect. Chemical agents kill or incapacitate people, destroy livestock or ravage crops. Some chemical agents are odorless and tasteless and are difficult to detect. They can have an immediate effect (a few seconds to a few minutes) or a delayed effect (several hours to several days). Biological and chemical weapons have been used primarily to terrorize an unprotected civilian population and not as a weapon of war. This is because of fear of retaliation and the likelihood that the agent would contaminate the battlefield for a long period of time. The Persian Gulf War in 1991 and other confrontations in the Middle East were causes for concern in the United States regarding the possibility of chemical or biological warfare. While no incidents occurred, there remains a concern that such weapons could be involved in an accident or be used by terrorists.

Terrorism in the United States

In the United States, most terrorist incidents have involved small extremist groups who use terrorism to achieve a designated objective. Local, State and Federal law enforcement officials monitor suspected terrorist groups and try to prevent or protect against a suspected attack. Additionally, the U.S. government works with other countries to limit the sources of support for terrorism. A terrorist attack can take several forms, depending on the technological means available to the terrorist, the nature of the political issue motivating the attack, and the points of weakness of the terrorist's target. Bombings are the most frequently used terrorist method in the United States. Other possibilities include an attack at transportation facilities, an attack against utilities or other public services or an incident involving chemical or biological agents. Terrorist incidents in this country have included bombings of the World Trade Center in New York City, the United States Capitol Building in Washington, D.C. and Mobil Oil corporate headquarters in New York City. The threat of terrorism has become very real. And the fear of terrorist acts has become even greater than the fear of crime. While it is foreign nationals that come to mind when we think about terrorism, Americans commit the majority of terrorist acts committed on American soil. For the nightclub security professional the same principles that are applied to preventing crime can be applied to preventing terrorist acts. The need for crime prevention has never been greater.

Following are some basic things nightclub/bar security can do:

- Teach security personnel to take steps to protect their club/bar, their patrons, and their fellow staff members.
- Teach security personnel to always be alert and aware of their surroundings.
- Encourage the logging and reporting of suspicious activity through appropriate channels.
- Stay alert to strange packages, boxes or bags left unattended for long periods of time in the club.
- Examine and inspect large handbags and knapsacks at the door.
- Create a liaison between your security, ABT and local law enforcement.

Develop a method to distribute information in the nightclub/bar that is fast and accurate in order to:

- o Create immediate awareness of potential dangers
- o Counteract false information and rumors that may be spreading
- o Reinforces teamwork and efficiency.

Prevention is the key ingredient to avoiding or minimizing disasters and tragedies. While it is difficult to show what specific disasters or tragedies never occurred or were minimized because of prevention, its impact can easily be measured through the reduction in crime, fire, and accident rates over the years. It makes this author proud to see fellow professionals in the trade doing their part to protect their country and citizens.

A "Massive" explosive device was found in a car in central London, laden with nails and propane gas canisters (according to reports from Sky News TV on Fox News Channel). Thankfully, alert bouncers at a nightclub spotted unusual activity across the street and notified authorities.

Suspected bomb found in London

Police have made safe a suspected car bomb in the heart of London. Officers carried out a controlled explosion after reports of a suspicious vehicle parked in The Haymarket shortly before 0200 BST (0100 GMT). The immediate area was cordoned off while police examined what they described as a "potentially viable explosive device". There are unconfirmed reports that gas canisters were removed from the back of the car, close to Piccadilly Circus. The government's emergency unit Cobra has called a meeting and the new Home Secretary Jacqui Smith is due to attend. One police source said the bomb was a "big device" and posed a real and substantial threat to the area around The Haymarket, which is in London's theatreland. A witness reported seeing gas canisters being removed from the car, believed to be a silver Mercedes, at around 0400 BST (O300 GMT). <u>Bouncers from a nearby nightclub said they saw the car being driven erratically before it crashed into a bin. They said the driver then got out and ran off. They called the police and reported the incident.</u>
Dozens of forensic officers were today poring over the scene, which was covered by a blue plastic police tent. Scotland Yard said detectives from Counter Terrorism Command were investigating the potential bomb plot and will be checking the CCTV in the area.

A spokesman said: "Police were called to reports of a suspicious vehicle parked in The Haymarket, shortly before 2am this morning. "As a precautionary measure the immediate area was cordoned off while explosives officers examined the vehicle.

"They discovered what appeared to be a potentially viable explosive device. This was made safe. Prime Minister Gordon Brown said the incident reminds us that Britain faces "a serious and continuous threat" and the public "need to be alert" at all times.

Chapter Nine:

Safety First!

Club Drugs, First-Aid & Fire Extinguishers

SERO IN PERICULIS EST CONSILIUM QUAERERE

'It's too late to ask for advice when the danger comes…'

Syrus, Maxims

Club Drugs

Across the country, teens and young adults enjoy all-night dance parties known as "raves" and increasingly encounter more than just music. Dangerous substances known collectively as club drugs - including Ecstasy, GHB, and Rohypnol-are gaining popularity. These drugs aren't "fun drugs." Although users may think these substances are harmless, research has shown that club drugs can produce a range of unwanted effects, including hallucinations, paranoia, amnesia, and in some cases, death. When used with alcohol, these drugs can be even more harmful. Some club drugs work on the same brain mechanisms as alcohol and, therefore, can dangerously boost the effects of both substances. Also, there are great differences among individuals in how they react to these substances and no one can predict how he or she will react. Some people have been known to have extreme, even fatal, reactions the first time they use club drugs. Studies suggest club drugs found in party settings are often adulterated or impure and thus even more dangerous. Because some club drugs are colorless, tasteless, and odorless, they are easy for people to slip into drinks. Some of these drugs have been associated with sexual assaults, and for that reason they are referred to as "date rape drugs."

An Introduction to Club Drugs

- "X," "Adam," and "Ecstasy" are slang names for **MDMA**, which is a stimulant and a hallucinogen. Young people may use Ecstasy to improve their moods or get energy to keep dancing; however, chronic abuse of MDMA appears to damage the brain's ability to think and regulate emotion, memory, sleep, and pain.

- "G," "Liquid Ecstasy," "Georgia Home Boy" or Gamma-hydroxybutyrate (**GHB**) may be made in homes by using recipes with common ingredients. At lower doses, GHB can relax the user, but, as the dose increases, the sedative effects may result in sleep and eventual coma or death.

- "Roofie" or "Roche" (**Rohypnol**) is tasteless and odorless. It mixes easily in carbonated beverages. Rohypnol may cause individuals under the influence of the drug to forget what happened. Other effects include low blood pressure, drowsiness, dizziness, confusion, and stomach upset.

- "Special K" or "K" (**Ketamine**) is an anesthetic. Use of a small amount of ketamine results in loss of attention span, learning ability, and memory. At higher doses, ketamine can cause delirium, amnesia, high blood pressure, depression, and severe breathing problems.

- "Speed," "Ice," "Chalk," "Meth" (**Methamphetamine**) is often made in home laboratories. Methamphetamine use can cause serious health concerns, including memory loss, aggression, violence, psychotic behavior, and heart problems.
- "Acid" or **Lysergic Acid Diethylamide (LSD)** may cause unpredictable behavior depending on the amount taken, where the drug is used, and on the user's personality. A user might feel the following effects: numbness, weakness, nausea, increased heart rate, sweating, and loss of appetite, "flashbacks," and sleeplessness.

Research Continues

"Raves" or all-night dance parties continue to attract teens and young adults who may think MDMA, GHB, Rohypnol, and other club drugs are harmless. This is not true. While researchers continue to study club drugs with a sense of urgency, treatment and prevention strategies are being developed. And the bottom line is simple: even experimenting with club drugs is an unpredictable and dangerous thing to do.

First-Aid & CPR

DISCLAIMER: <u>Under no conditions will responsibility be accepted by the author, or anyone else related to this manual regarding the consequences of use of the chapter distributed in this documentation in any First Aid application.</u>

*<u>THIS IS A STUDY AID, NOT A FIRST AID MANUAL.</u>

Introduction

Universally, one of the biggest weaknesses that nightclub security possess, is the lack of training when it comes to emergency first aid. You may encounter door personnel that have resumes that describe them as experienced security specialists: hand to hand combat experienced, threat assessment, de-escalation skills, interviewing procedures, report writing, false identification training and communication skills. However, when

asking a doorman if they have first aid training, 90% give you a blank stare.

Emergency first aid is not only a great tool to possess for your tool

box but many employers or insurance companies require staff to have this

type of training. Nightclub security is on the front line so to speak and it makes sense that these are the people that have the knowledge and skills to attend to injured patrons. Remember, the door staff are usually the first on the scene when it comes to injuries. It makes sense then that these employees should have some type of emergency first aid training. This training will include knowledge in these areas: broken limb immobilization, CPR, wounds and bleeding, signs of shock, C spin control (neck and spine injuries), and recovery position (in case of vomiting) and other types of emergency first aid procedures. Most employers will be happy to certify a core group of their employees. The law usually requires that at least one staff member on site must have emergency first aid and CPR. It should be noted that just because one possesses these skills, one is not required to use them. If certain situations make administering first aid or CPR dangerous, then the First aid attendant usually won't be held liable.

These situations may include:
- No gloves or mask when attending to a person,
- An angry mob or violent situation,
- Hazardous material or situation (fire)
- A situation that exceeds that knowledge of the first aid responder.

Remember, first aid doesn't mean that you have to be able to perform surgery; it means that you are the person who can stabilize a patient, until medical help arrives. This also may include just sitting with an injured person and talking with them. Having a calm and caring voice talking with you when you are injured goes a long way.

This chapter has been reviewed by a Certified First Aid Instructor with many years experience teaching first aid, CPR and basic life support courses. While the material presented conforms to commonly accepted standards, it is not intended to substitute for formalized classroom instruction in first aid, as offered by many community groups and organizations. Nor should this chapter be relied upon solely for use at the time of an emergency. **The time to learn first aid is BEFORE you need to use it!** Each year 64 million Americans sustain injuries that require medical attention or restrict their activities for more than half-a-day! The material in this chapter could save the life of someone dear to you! We suggest you read the material to get an overview of the various areas covered, then spend time reviewing each topic in detail.

Since you will probably use the skills presented in this chapter only from time to time, it is a good idea to review its content every so often so you don't forget the valuable lessons.

<u>*This author strongly recommends you sign up for an inclusive first aid and CPR course.</u>

Your 'Personal' First Aid Kit

Everyone should have a well-stocked 'Locking' First Aid Kit when working the door. <u>Having it locked will prevent it from being raided by fellow employees.</u> The contents of your kit will vary depending upon the number of people it is designed to protect as well as special circumstances where it will be used. For example, a first aid kit in a factory where there may be danger of flying debris getting into the eye should certainly have a sterile eyewash solution in its kit. If a family member is a known diabetic, your kit at home should have a glucose, or sugar solution.

When assembling your first aid kit, you should consider possible injuries you are likely to encounter and then select kit contents to treat those conditions. It's also important to check your kit periodically to restock items that have been used and to replace items that are out-of-date.

Recommended Contents for a First Aid Kit

[Modify to suit your particular needs]

- Activated Charcoal (for poisoning emergencies)
- Adhesive strip bandages - assorted sizes Adhesive tape
- Alcohol - rubbing 70%
- Alcohol wipes
- Antacid
- Antibiotic ointment
- Baking soda
- Calamine lotion
- Chemical ice packs
- Chemical hot packs
- Cotton balls
- Cotton swabs
- Decongestant tablets & spray
- Diarrhea medication
- Disposable latex or vinyl gloves
- Elastic bandages
- Face mask for CPR

- Flashlight
- Gauze pads - various sizes
- Hot-water bottle
- Household ammonia
- Hydrocortisone cream .5%
- Hydrogen Peroxide
- Hypoallergenic tape
- Ice bag
- Insect repellent
- Insect sting swabs
- Matches
- Meat tenderizer (for insect bites)
- Moleskin
- Needles
- Non-adhering dressings [Telfa]
- Oil of Cloves
- Over-the-counter pain medication [aspirin]
- Paper & pencil
- Paper drinking cups
- Roller gauze - self adhering
- Safety pins
- Salt
- Scissors
- Soap
- Space blanket
- Sam splint

- Sugar or glucose solution
- Syrup of Ipecac
- Thermometer - oral
- Tongue blades
- Triangular bandages
- Tweezers
- Waterproof tape

Legal and Ethical Considerations

DUTY TO ACT

No one is required to render first aid under normal circumstances. Even a physician could ignore a stranger suffering a heart attack if he chose to do so. Exceptions include situations where a person's employment designates the rendering of first aid as a part of described job duties. Examples include lifeguards, law enforcement officers, park rangers and safety officers in industry. A duty to provide first aid also exists where an individual has presumed responsibility for another person's safety, as in the case of a security professional-patron, security professional-staff, bodyguard-client or parent-child. While in most cases there is no legal responsibility to provide first aid care to another person, there is a very clear responsibility to continue care once you start. You cannot start first aid and then stop unless the victim no longer needs your attention, other first aiders take over the responsibility from you, or you are physically unable to continue care.

NEED FOR CONSENT

In every instance where first aid is to be provided, the victim's consent is required. It should be obtained from every conscious, mentally competent adult. The consent may be either oral or written. Permission to render first aid to an unconscious victim is implied and a first aider should not hesitate to treat an unconscious victim. Consent of a parent or guardian is required to treat a child, however emergency first aid necessary to maintain life may be provided without such consent.

IT IS IMPORTANT TO REMEMBER THAT A VICTIM HAS THE RIGHT TO REFUSE FIRST AID CARE AND IN THESE INSTANCES YOU MUST RESPECT THE VICTIM'S DECISION. YOU CANNOT FORCE CARE
ON A PERSON WHO DOES NOT WANT IT ... REGARDLESS OF THEIR CONDITION!

LEGAL CONCERNS

Some well-meaning people hesitate to provide first aid because they are concerned about being sued. This need not be a concern! Legislators in almost every state in the country have passed the **GOOD SAMARITAN LAW,** which is intended to protect good people who offer first aid help to others.

Most of the Good Samaritan Acts are very similar in their content and usually provide two basic requirements, which must be met in order for the first aider to be protected by their provisions:

The first aider must not deliberately cause harm to the victim.

The first aider must provide the level & type of care expected of a reasonable person with the same amount of training & in similar circumstances.

*THERE SHOULD BE LITTLE, IF ANY, CONCERN ABOUT LEGAL CONSEQUENCES INHERENT IN PROVIDING FIRST AID. YOU NEED ONLY HAVE THE VICTIM'S CONSENT AND THEN OFFER THE LEVEL OF CARE FOR WHICH YOU ARE QUALIFIED.

Order of Priority in an Emergency

In EVERY emergency situation, there is a logical order to be followed. First, it is important to carefully assess the scene of an emergency BEFORE any further steps are taken. The purpose of this assessment is to assure it is safe to provide first aid care. For example, an unconscious victim might be lying on a live power line. If a rescuer were to touch the victim before the power could be shut off, the rescuer would become a victim as well! Always be sure it is safe before you attempt to help a victim!

SECURE THE ACCIDENT SCENE FIRST!

Once you determine it is safe for you to help a victim, you should immediately determine if the victim has any life threatening conditions.

Begin by checking to see if the victim is responsive. Kneel and ask, "ARE YOU OK?" If there is no response, you must immediately summon an ambulance! Recent studies have conclusively shown that victims who are not breathing and do not have a heartbeat have a substantially greater chance for survival if they receive prompt advanced medical care in a hospital or by trained paramedics. Only after a call is placed for emergency medical services does a volunteer attempt to further help an unconscious victim. If there are bystanders on the scene, summon someone to your side to provide assistance. If the victim is on his stomach, first place the victim's arm closest to you above his head. Then turn him over by placing one hand on the victim's hip and the other hand at the victim's shoulder. Turn the body in a smooth, even straight line so as to not cause further injury in the event of existing spinal cord injury. With the victim now on his back, OPEN THE VICTIM'S AIRWAY by placing the heel of your hand on the victim's forehead and the tips of your fingers under the bony part of the jaw. Push down on the forehead while lifting up the chin until the jaw is pointing straight up. Now place your ear over the victim's mouth and LOOK, LISTEN, and FEEL for breathing for 3 to 5 seconds. LOOK at the chest to see if it is rising, LISTEN for sounds of breathing and FEEL for air coming from the victim.

IF THE VICTIM IS NOT BREATHING, RESCUE BREATHING IS REQUIRED IMMEDIATELY!

IMPORTANT

WHILE THIS CHAPTER IDENTIFIES LIFE THREATENING CONDITIONS REQUIRING RESCUE BREATHING OR CPR, THESE SKILLS REQUIRE INTENSIVE CLASSROOM SKILL DEVELOPMENT AND PRACTICE AND CANNOT BE EFFECTIVELY PRESENTED OR TAUGHT IN THIS CHAPTER. THE AUTHOR STRONGLY ENCOURAGES EVERYONE TO ENROLL IN A CPR COURSE

Rescue breathing will provide vital oxygen to a victim who cannot breathe on their own. After giving the victim two breaths, the pulse is checked at the Carotid Artery to ascertain if the victim has a heartbeat. This artery is located on the side of the neck and is found by first positioning the fingers on the victim's Adam's Apple, then sliding the fingers down into the soft groove on the side of the neck. The pulse is checked for 5 to 10 seconds.

If the victim has a heartbeat, but is not breathing, RESCUE BREATHING is required. If the victim is NOT breathing AND does NOT have a HEARTBEAT, CPR is required without delay!

These initial steps of checking the AIRWAY, BREATHING and CIRCULATION (pulse), together with a check for major BLEEDING, constitute THE PRIMARY SURVEY, which looks for life-threatening conditions! In every instance where first aid is to be provided, it is important to always ask a conscious victim for permission to help them. If a victim is unconscious, it is presumed they have provided consent for you to assist them.

Obstructions in the Airway

NOTE: Emergency treatment of airway obstructions is taught as part of CPR training and only through classroom practice can the necessary skills be mastered. The mechanics of handling airway obstructions are presented in this chapter for background insight only.

If an individual is choking - but can speak or cough forcibly - there is an exchange of air (although it might be diminished) and you should encourage the victim to continue coughing while you just stand by! On the other hand, if a victim is choking, but CANNOT speak or cough, an airway obstruction exists which must be treated immediately!

The treatment for an obstructed airway in a conscious victim involves use of the **HEIMLICH MANEUVER**, which is performed as follows:

- Stand behind the victim.
- Wrap your arms around the victim's waist.
- Make a fist with one hand and place the thumb side of the fist against the victim's abdomen just above the navel and well below the lower tip of the breastbone.
- Grasp your fist with your other hand, with elbows out, and press your fist into the victim's abdomen with quick, upward thrusts.
- Each thrust is a distinct, separate attempt to dislodge the foreign object.
- Repeat thrusts until foreign object is cleared or the victim becomes unconscious.

Emergency treatment of airway obstructions in an unconscious victim is taught in CPR classes.

Heart Attack

Heart attacks are among the leading cause of death in the United States. A heart attack happens when one or more of the blood vessels that supply blood to the heart become blocked. When this occurs, cells in the heart begin to die when they cannot get blood for vital nourishment. If a large part of the heart is deprived of blood, the heart stops beating and the victim suffers CARDIAC ARREST!

When a victim's heart stops beating, they require CARDIOPULMONARY RESUSCITATION (CPR) which provides vital oxygen through rescue breathing and which maintains circulation through chest compressions.

PROPER TRAINING IS REQUIRED TO PERFORM CPR, HOWEVER ANY HEART ATTACK CAN LEAD TO CARDIAC ARREST AND IT IS THEREFORE VITAL FOR FIRST AIDERS TO BE ABLE TO RECOGNIZE THE EARLY WARNING SIGNS OF A HEART ATTACK SO THE VICTIM CAN RECEIVE PROMPT PROFESSIONAL ATTENTION!

A heart attack victim whose heart is still beating has a much better chance of survival than a victim whose heart has stopped! Most heart attack victims who die succumb within 2 hours after having their heart attack. Many of these victims could be saved if bystanders recognize the symptoms of a heart attack and get the victim to a hospital quickly! Indeed, many victims of heart attacks think they are experiencing HEARTBURN or other minor discomfort when in fact their life is in jeopardy! The most significant sign of a heart attack is chest pain. The victim may describe it as pressure, a feeling of tightness in the chest, aching, crushing, fullness or tightness, constricting or heavy pain. The pain may be located in the center of the chest although it is not uncommon for the pain to radiate to one or both shoulders or arms or to the neck, jaw or back. In addition to pain, victims may experience sweating, nausea or shortness of breath. Many victims deny they may be having a heart attack. Others may have their condition worsened by fear of dying.

With all victims of heart attacks - and with all victims receiving first aid for any condition - it is important for the rescuer to constantly reassure the victim and keep them as calm and relaxed as possible.

The psychological value of reassurance is as important in first aid as any treatments!

FIRST AID FOR A HEART ATTACK:

- Recognize the signs & symptoms of a heart attack
- Comfort & reassure the victim
- Have the victim stop whatever they were doing and sit or lie in a comfortable position
- Summon emergency medical help quickly
- If the victim becomes unconscious, be prepared to perform CPR [IF YOU ARE TRAINED TO DO SO]
- All of us can reduce the risk of heart attack by controlling high blood pressure, limiting cholesterol in the diet, watching weight, exercising, giving up smoking and minimizing stress.

Bleeding

Major bleeding may be a life-threatening condition requiring immediate attention. Bleeding may be external or internal. Bleeding may be from an ARTERY, a major blood vessel that carries oxygen-rich blood from the heart throughout the body. It may be from a VEIN, which carries blood back to the heart to be oxygenated or bleeding may be from a CAPILLARY, the smallest of our body's blood vessels.

ARTERIAL bleeding is characterized by spurts with each beat of the heart, is bright red in color (although blood darkens when it meets the air) and is usually severe and hard to control. ARTERIAL bleeding requires immediate attention!

VENUS bleeding is characterized by a steady flow and the blood is dark, almost maroon in shade. Venus bleeding is easier to control than Arterial bleeding.

CAPILLARY bleeding is usually slow, oozing in nature and this type of bleeding usually has a higher risk of infection than other types of bleeding.

FIRST AID FOR BLEEDING IS INTENDED TO:
- STOP THE BLEEDING
- PREVENT INFECTION
- PREVENT SHOCK

How to control bleeding
Apply DIRECT PRESSURE on the wound. use a dressing, if available. If a dressing is not available, use a rag, towel, piece of clothing or your hand alone.
* **IMPORTANT:** ONCE PRESSURE IS APPLIED, KEEP IT IN PLACE. IF DRESSINGS BECOME SOAKED WITH BLOOD, APPLY NEW DRESSINGS OVER THE OLD DRESSINGS. THE LESS A BLEEDING WOUND IS DISTURBED; THE EASIER IT WILL BE TO STOP THE BLEEDING!
If bleeding continues, and you do not suspect a fracture, ELEVATE the wound above the level of the heart and continue to apply direct pressure.

If the bleeding still cannot be controlled, the next step is to apply PRESSURE AT A PRESSURE POINT. For wounds of the arms or hands, pressure points are located on the inside of the wrist (radial artery-where a pulse is checked) or on the inside of the upper arm (brachial artery). For wounds of the legs, the pressure point is at the crease in the groin (femoral artery). Steps 1 and 2 should be continued with use of the pressure points.

The final step to control bleeding is to apply a PRESSURE BANDAGE over the wound. Note the distinction between a dressing and a bandage. A dressing may be a gauze square applied directly to a wound, while a bandage, such as roll gauze, is used to hold a dressing in place. Pressure should be used in applying the bandage. After the bandage is in place, it is important to check the pulse to make sure circulation is not interrupted. When faced with the need to control major bleeding, it is not important that the dressings you will use are sterile! Use whatever you have at hand and work fast!

* A SLOW PULSE RATE, OR BLUISH-PURPLE FINGERTIPS OR TOES,
SIGNAL A BANDAGE MAY BE IMPEDING CIRCULATION.

Signs and symptoms of INTERNAL BLEEDING are:

- Bruised, swollen, tender or rigid abdomen
- Bruises on chest are signs of fractured ribs
- Blood in vomit
- Wounds that have penetrated the chest or abdomen

- Bleeding from the rectum or vagina

- Abnormal pulse and difficulty breathing

- Cool, moist skin

First aid in the field for internal bleeding is limited. If the injury appears to be a simple bruise, apply cold packs to slow bleeding, relieve pain and reduce swelling. If you suspect more severe internal bleeding, carefully monitor the patient and be prepared to administer CPR if required (and you are trained to do so). You should also reassure the victim, control external bleeding, care for shock (covered in next section), loosen tight-fitting clothing and place victim on side so fluids can drain from the mouth.

Shock

SHOCK is common with many injuries, regardless of their severity. The first hour after an injury is most important because it is during this period that symptoms of shock appear.

* IF SHOCK IS NOT TREATED, IT CAN PROGRESS TO CAUSE DEATH!
ANY TYPE OF INJURY CAN CAUSE SHOCK.

Shock is failure of the cardiovascular system to keep adequate blood circulating to the vital organs of the body, namely the heart, lungs and brain.

SIGNS AND SYMPTOMS OF SHOCK INCLUDE: confused behavior, very fast or very slow pulse rate, very fast or very slow breathing, trembling and weakness in the arms or legs, cool and moist skin, pale or bluish skin, lips and fingernails and enlarged pupils.

Treatment for Shock

A good rule to follow is to anticipate that shock will follow an injury and to take measures to prevent it before it happens.

Putting a victim in a lying-down position improves circulation.

If the victim is not suspected of having head or neck injuries, or leg fractures, elevate the legs.

If you suspect head or neck injuries, keep the victim lying flat. If the victim vomits, turn them on their side.

If victim is experiencing trouble breathing, place them in a semi-reclining position. Maintain the victim's body temperature, but do not overheat.

Burns

The severity of a burn depends upon its size, depth and location. Burns are most severe when located on the face, neck, hands, feet and genitals. Also, when they are spread over large parts of the body or when they are combined with other injuries.

Burns result in pain, infection and shock. They are most serious when the victims are very young or very old.

FIRST DEGREE burns are the least severe. They are characterized by redness or discoloration, mild swelling and pain. Overexposure to the sun is a common cause of first-degree burns.

SECOND DEGREE burns are more serious. They are deeper than first degree burns, look red or mottled and have blisters. They may also involve loss of fluids through the damaged skin. Second-degree burns are usually the most painful because nerve ending are usually intact, despite severe tissue damage.

THIRD DEGREE burns are the deepest. They may look white or charred, extend through all skin layers. Victims of third degree burns may have severe pain -- or no pain at all -- if the nerve endings are destroyed.

First Aid for Burns

- FIRST DEGREE: Flush with cool running water, Apply moist dressings and bandage loosely.
- SECOND DEGREE: Apply dry dressings and bandage loosely-Do not use water as it may increase risk of shock.
- THIRD DEGREE: Same treatment as second degree.

ALL VICTIMS OF SERIOUS BURNS
SHOULD SEEK PROFESSIONAL HELP QUICKLY!

CHEMICALS may also cause Burns. In these cases, it is important to remove clothing on which chemicals have spilled and flush the affected area with copious amounts of water for 15 to 30 minutes.

Eye Injuries

Be extremely careful and gentle when treating eye injuries.

Floating objects in the eye, which can be visualized, may be flushed from the eye with water. If the object cannot be removed in this manner, the victim should seek medical attention.

NEVER ATTEMPT TO REMOVE OBJECTS EMBEDDED IN THE EYE!

First Aid care for these injuries consists of bandaging BOTH eyes and seeking professional care promptly!

An inverted paper cup covered with a bandage is appropriate for serious eye injuries while the victim is transported to the hospital.

For chemical burns of the eye, wash the eye with copious amounts of water for 15 to 30 minutes. Then wrap a bandage around both eyes and seek professional help. Eyes are delicate and sight is precious! Prompt professional attention to eye injuries is required to preserve sight!

Nose Injuries

Severe nosebleed can be most frightening. It can also lead to shock if enough blood is lost! Many cases of nosebleed can be controlled simply by having the victim sit down, pinch the nostrils shut and lean forward (to prevent blood from running into the throat).

Once the bleeding has been stopped, talking, walking and blowing the nose may disturb blood clots and allow the bleeding to resume. The victim should rest quietly until it appears the bleeding remains stopped.

If it is suspected that the victim has suffered head, neck or back injuries DO NOT attempt to control the blood flow as they may cause increased pressure on injured tissue. All uncontrolled nosebleeds require prompt medical attention!

Fractures, Sprains, Strains & Dislocations

Fractures, sprains, strains and dislocations may be hard for the layperson to tell apart. For this reason, first aid treatment of any of these conditions is handled as though the injury was a fracture. Signs and symptoms of the above conditions may include a "grating" sensation of bones rubbing together, pain, tenderness, swelling, bruising and an inability to move the injured part.

First Aid for any of these conditions consists of:

- Control bleeding, if present.
- Care for shock.
- Splint affected area to prevent further movement, but do so only if possible without causing further pain to victim.
- Cold packs may help reduce pain and swelling.
- Victims with traumatic injuries, such as those caused by automobile accidents, falls etc. should not be moved except by trained rescue workers.

- Head, neck and back injuries are serious and require special care for movement and transport of victims with these conditions. In exceptional circumstances, such as when a victim is at risk of further injury unless moved, the victim's head and neck should be stabilized and the body moved with minimal flexing of the head, neck or spinal cord.

ALL VICTIMS WITH FRACTURES, DISLOCATIONS, SPRAINS AND STRAINS REQUIRE PROFESSIONAL MEDICAL ATTENTION.

Poisoning

Over a million cases of poisoning occur in the United States each year, most involving young children.

PREVENTION of poisoning should be the concern of every parent with young children. Substances likely to cause poisoning should be kept away from inquiring youngsters! Since various poisons cause different symptoms, and because treatments vary depending upon the substance ingested, the first step in the event of poisoning is to call the local POISON CONTROL CENTER!

DO NOT WAIT FOR SYMPTOMS TO OCCUR!
IDENTIFY THE NATURE OF THE POISON AND RECEIVE SPECIFIC CARE INSTRUCTIONS FROM THE PROFESSIONAL STAFF AT THE CENTER!

All poisoning victims need to be monitored carefully for signs of shock or impaired consciousness. Every household should keep ACTIVATED CHARCOAL & SYRUP OF IPECAC on hand for possible use in poisoning emergencies, however they should not be administered unless instructed by the Poison Control Center staff. Both of these items are readily available, without prescription, at any drug store.

Stroke

Stroke occurs when the blood flow to the brain is interrupted long enough to cause damage. This may be caused by a clot formed in an artery in the brain or carried to the brain in the bloodstream, a ruptured artery in the brain or by compression of an artery in the brain, as found with brain tumors   Signs and symptoms of a stroke include:

- Weakness and numbness of the face, arm or leg, often on one side of the body only.
- Dizziness
- Confusion
- Headache
- Ringing in the ears
- A change of mood
- Difficulty speaking
- Unconsciousness
- Pupils of uneven size
- Difficulty in breathing and swallowing
- Loss of bowel and bladder control

IF YOU SUSPECT A PERSON IS HAVING A STROKE, HAVE THEM STOP WHATEVER THEY ARE DOING AND REST.

PROMPTLY OBTAIN PROFESSIONAL HELP.

Reassure the victim and keep them comfortable. Do not give anything by mouth. If the victim vomits, allow for fluids to drain from the mouth. Observe carefully while awaiting professional help and, if trained to do so, monitor the airway, breathing and circulation and BE PREPARED TO ADMINISTER RESCUE BREATHING OR CPR, IF REQUIRED!

Seizure

SEIZURES are fairly common occurrences, but are very misunderstood! Seizures, per se, are not a specific condition. Rather, many different types of conditions such as insulin shock, high fevers, viral infections of the brain, head injuries or drug reactions may cause them. When seizures recur with no identifiable cause, the person is said to have epilepsy.

Signs and Symptoms

Many individuals have a warning AURA (or sensation) before the onset of a seizure. Many times, a person about to have a seizure will physically move themselves from danger (as from the edge of a train platform) before the seizure begins. Seizures can range from mild to severe. Mild seizures may take place and end in a matter of seconds. Severe seizures may involve uncontrollable muscle spasms, rigidity, loss of consciousness, loss of bladder and bowel control, and in some cases, breathing that stops temporarily. Many epileptics carry cards or bracelets, which identify their condition.

First Aid

Summon professional help. Prevent the person from injuring him or herself by moving furniture or equipment.

DO NOT ATTEMPT TO RESTRAIN A PERSON SUFFERING A SEIZURE AND DO NOT PUT ANYTHING IN THEIR MOUTH!

Loosen clothing. If they vomit, turn on their side to allow fluids to drain. Stay with the person until they are fully conscious. If trained, administer rescue breathing or CPR, if required.

Fire Extinguishers

This author has so much respect for the dangers of fire hazards that I have devoted several pages of this chapter to explain it.

* A bouncer/doorman should always check Fire Exits and inspect the Fire Extinguishers ever night before his or her shift starts. This author cannot reiterate this very important procedure enough!

In 95% of Nightclubs and Bars you will find ABC class Fire extinguishers.

There are basically four different types or classes of fire extinguishers, each of which extinguishes specific types of fire. Newer fire extinguishers use a picture/labeling system to designate which types of fires they are to be used on. Older fire extinguishers are labeled with colored geometrical shapes with letter designations. Both of these types of labels are shown below with the description of the different classes of extinguishers.

Additionally, Class A and Class B fire extinguishers have a numerical rating which is based on tests conducted by Underwriter's Laboratories that are designed to determine the extinguishing potential for each size and type of extinguisher.

Fire Extinguisher Ratings

Class A Extinguishers will put out fires in ordinary combustibles, such as wood and paper. The numerical rating for this class of fire extinguisher refers to the amount of water the fire extinguisher holds and the amount of fire it will extinguish.

Ordinary Combustibles

Class B Extinguishers should be used on fires involving flammable liquids, such as grease, gasoline, oil, etc. The numerical rating for this class of fire extinguisher states the approximate number of square feet of a flammable liquid fire that a non-expert person can expect to extinguish.

Flammable Liquids

Class C Extinguishers are suitable for use on electrically energized fires. This class of fire extinguishers does not have a numerical rating. The presence of the letter "C" indicates that the extinguishing agent is non-conductive.

Electrical Equipment

Class D Extinguishers are designed for use on flammable metals and are often specific for the type of metal in question. There is no picture designator for Class D extinguishers. These extinguishers generally have no rating nor are they given a multi-purpose rating for use on other types of fires.

D

Combustible
Metals

Multi-Class Ratings

Many extinguishers available today can be used on different types of fires and will be labeled with more than one designator, e.g. A-B, B-C, or A-B-C. Make sure that if you have a multi-purpose extinguisher it is properly labeled.

This is the old style of labeling indicating suitability for use on Class A, B, and C fires.

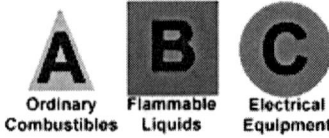

This is the new style of labeling that shows this extinguisher may be used on Ordinary Combustibles, Flammable Liquids, or Electrical Equipment fires. This is the new labeling style with a diagonal red line drawn through the picture to indicate what type of fire this extinguisher is NOT suitable for. In this example, the fire extinguisher could be used on Ordinary Combustibles and Flammable Liquids fires, but not for Electrical Equipment fires.

How to Use a Fire Extinguisher

Even though extinguishers come in a number of shapes and sizes, they all operate in a similar manner. Here's an easy acronym for fire extinguisher use:

P A S S -- Pull, Aim, Squeeze, and Sweep

Pull the pin at the top of the extinguisher that keeps the handle from being accidentally pressed.

Aim the nozzle toward the base of the fire.

Stand approximately 8 feet away from the fire and squeeze the handle to discharge the extinguisher. If you release the handle, the discharge will stop. Sweep the nozzle back and forth at the base of the fire. After the fire appears to be out, watch it carefully since it may re-ignite!

Chapter Ten:

The Law & the Nightclub Security Professional

LEGES BONAE EX MALIS MORIBUS PROCREANTUR

'Good laws are produced by bad morals..'

Macrobius, Saturnalia II, 13

By
Dan R. Miller, Ph.D.
Bethune-Cookman University

Introduction

Although you don't have to be a lawyer to stay within the law and still be effective in nightclub security, there are some basic concepts that you have to know. I am going to present them to you here. If you understand these basics, you can apply them to just about any situation you encounter, and know the right thing to do. Most people are afraid of the law. They fear getting sued and they back away from doing what they should. But the law works both ways. Not only can you get sued for what you do, but you can also be held accountable for what you fail to do. Knowledge of the law will remove this fear so you can do your job, legally, professionally and effectively. You have responsibilities but you also have authority and rights. When you get finished reading this chapter you will know what they are.

There are 3 types of Law: Civil, Criminal and Administrative.

Civil

Civil Law is concerned with problems between individuals. It encompasses losses or damages because of something you did, that you were not supposed to do, or because of something you didn't do that you should have done.

Generally we are talking about the plaintiff (customer) convincing the judge
that you, your boss, his boss, your company, and your insurance carrier, should pay him a lot of money.

As far as nightclub security is concerned, civil law is about money, not jail time.

The legal theories of "deep pockets" and Vicarious Liability apply to civil law cases. The Plaintiff (the customer) and his lawyer want to go after the people with the most money, those with the deepest pockets. That's why they name everyone they can in the suit, to make sure they find someone with money or insurance. You can't get money from a stone.

Vicarious liability means that an employer is responsible for the actions of his employees. There are some limitations but it is very difficult for an employer to be held blameless, when his or her employees do wrong.

The major tort (civil wrong) that plaintiffs sue for is negligence. This is not mere carelessness or inattention. It must be some seriously wrong action or inaction that can closely be tied to the loss. Sometimes, owners are sued for hiring someone negligently, because the applicant had a background of assaults, sexual offenses or whatever. The employer may not have checked, or he may think that people who have a history of violence make good bouncers.

Negligent training is another target. Some nightclubs just hire big guys in muscle shirts, who have no idea about the real responsibilities of a bouncer. They don't know anything about the professional techniques you learn in this book or one of our classes. They are not going to do things right because they don't know what right is.

They just haven't been taught. This situation virtually guarantees that the plaintiff (customer) will win the case, or that the owner or insurance company will have to settle, because their potential risk of losing is too great. Invariably, the bouncer will be asked to describe the formal training he has. Judges and juries don't react well when the witness (you) answers this question with the word "none."

If someone sues a nightclub, many times the club owner quickly pays him or her off, especially if the owner knows his security is in the wrong. The owner looks at it as just another cost of doing business. This is common practice in nightclubs/bars where the security has a reputation for being violent and unprofessional. Committing torts (civil wrongs) and crimes (violations of criminal law) carry significant risk for both owner and employee. Judges and juries tend to side with the customer in these cases. It is ludicrous to put security people on the floor without any documented formal training. Judges and juries award 'big money' to customers for such outrageous lack of regard for the their safety. If owners don't insure that their security are properly selected and trained, that they know what to do and when to do it, they are seriously negligent. Everyone is held responsible, from the bouncer/doorman on up to the owner or corporation and their insurance company. Corporations are considered persons for the purposes of civil and criminal law, and can be brought to court to answer for their actions and those of their employees.

Just as civil law is concerned with what happened between individuals, for example, Jones vs. Smith, criminal law is concerned with wrongs against society, for example, The State vs. Jones.

What ever happened between Jones and Smith is a personal matter, between them, and the rest of us are really not involved.

In a criminal wrong, known as a crime, society has been harmed. It has been said that the fabric of society is torn when a crime is committed. Burglaries in our neighborhoods and rapes in our city affect us all. Crime interferes with our ability to pursue or enjoy our daily activities. In the example of wrongdoing mentioned earlier in this chapter, ask yourself if the bouncers committed a crime or a tort? The answer is both. Remember O.J Simpson? He was acquitted of the crime and then was sued for the same action civilly, as a tort. As we know, he lost the civil case and was ordered to pay the plaintiffs millions of dollars. Again, you can't get money from a stone.

Civil and criminal court jurisdictions are separate, and actions can be brought in both, without violating the constitutional protection against double jeopardy.

You probably already know this but for the sake of completeness I will repeat it below:

There are two kinds of crimes: <u>Felonies</u> and <u>Misdemeanors</u>

Serious crimes are designated as felonies. Conviction of a felony can disqualify a person from certain benefits of citizenship.
Less serious crimes are designated misdemeanors, they include Shoplifting, minor assaults, illegal gambling, prostitution, trespass, damage to property, etc.

Now that you have a basic foundation in the law, as it affects nightclub security, we will look at the legal aspects of using force.

The Use of Force

Generally, although this is slowly changing in some states, security personnel <u>have the same rights and authority as any ordinary citizen and no more.</u> A citizen has the right to defend himself but may only use the <u>minimum amount of force necessary to accomplish this and no more.</u>

A citizen or nightclub security person, may use the minimum amount of force necessary to protect himself or a customer who is in imminent danger of bodily injury. If you exceed this standard, you're probably in trouble. Deadly force, the force likely to cause death or serious bodily injury, may <u>only</u> be used to defend yourself or another from imminent serious bodily injury or death.

 This is known as the <u>Defense of Life Standard</u>. Deadly force may never be used to protect money or property, no matter how valuable. Any time you use force, the police should be called to respond.

Remember, you are only authorized to go to the minimum level required by the circumstances.

The Law of Citizen's Arrest

Nightclub security personnel are not granted any special powers of arrest other than those of an ordinary citizen.
The common law principal of citizen's arrest is familiar to most people, but less familiar is what the law actually entails. Before law was written down society operated under the principle of common law. Common law evolved through the decisions of those hearing cases.

Rather than decide similar cases over and over again, society recognized that whatever decisions the judges made would apply to subsequent cases, so this became the law. Eventually they decided to codify (write down) the law, and that is the status of the law we have today. Common law provided that a common citizen could arrest someone who was committing a felony in his or her presence. Citizen's arrests rarely occur because the felon usually has the upper hand, making it foolhardy for the citizen to act.

Remember, you are only authorized to go to the minimum level required by the circumstances.

The legal concepts of The Reasonable Man Standard and the Totality of The Circumstances are used by judges and juries to help them decide where on the SAR Matrix you were justified in being.

The Reasonable Man Standard determines whether a person of good judgment would have felt justified in doing what you did. Monday morning quarterbacking is not permitted, but only the facts known to you at the time can be considered. Also, the Totality of the Circumstances concept requires that all of the factors involved must be used in the reasonable man decision, not just an isolated action, by itself.

Trespass

Trespass is defined as remaining on an owner's property after being told to leave by the property owner or his agent [You].

The legal basis for ejecting patrons from a bar or nightclub sometimes comes into question. Here is another case in which you derive your authority from citizen's rights. The citizen has certain property owner's rights and these pass onto you, his agent.

The property owner can exclude persons who do not follow his or her reasonable rules and regulations. Once the property owner or his agent has ordered someone to leave the premises they are legally required to do so or they are trespassing.

At this point the owner or his agent (you) may use force to end the trespass.

The property owner (or you, as his agent) can also use force to prevent the trespass from occurring.

Remember, if you are involved in a use of force situation, your actions would be illegal if you used more force than was necessary to accomplish your legal objective.

Again whenever you use force it MUST be the minimum amount necessary.

Administrative Law

Administrative law contains the rules, regulations and procedures that the state has adopted to regulate an industry. In our case these are the alcohol beverage control laws, which are administered by the Alcohol Beverage Commission, a state agency.

The main involvement of nightclub security personnel in administrative law relates to checking for underage patrons. Procedures and safeguards for checking I.D. were presented previously in this book.

A Final Word…

Initial training and updating skills are the "mark" of a true professional. This "mark" can save you, your supervisor, and everyone up to and including your owner, from very serious legal problems.

Imagine the jury's reaction when you take the witness stand and are asked the inevitable question "Tell me about your formal training in night club security ". If you had little or none, I would be surprised if your attorney continued the trial and didn't try to settle. How can you do something right if you don't have the proper training to know what right is and how do it correctly? How can the judge or jury believe that you or your employer cared about the safety of your patrons, when no one bothered to train security personnel how to safely and legally handle potentially volatile situations? Prevention and de-escalation are much better techniques than force. That's why these preventive methods are taught in our classes and this book. Follow what you have learned in this chapter and you will be a professional nightclub security person who will be well protected from legal problems.

MAKE SURE YOUR ACTIONS ARE LEGAL, ETHICAL, MORAL AND RESPONSIBLE AND THAT YOU ARE ACTING IN GOOD FAITH WITHOUT MALICE OR PERSONAL REVENGE MOTIVES.

Canadian Laws

Each province has their own liquor act in Canada. Here is an example of an act from British Columbia. Just type in your search terms "Liquor Act + Law + "your province" and you should be directed to the proper governmental web page. Typically, the liquor laws in Canada fall under the LCLB (Liquor Control and Licensing Branch). In the States, it is usually called the ABT or ABC. While the science of bouncing has commonalities that cross boarders, the actual liquor laws do change drastically from state to state, province to province, and country to country. For example, a bouncer working a nightclub in Las Vegas wouldn't bat an eye at someone drinking outside his or her door or on the strip. However, local authorities may fine a doorman in Vancouver, Canada if this was to occur. How then do we cover an act that is so different in so many places? The answer is that we can't. But getting to know your liquor act is an essential piece of information that can PROTECT you from harm. Knowing your rights gives you the knowledge on how to operate within certain boundaries. I'll give you some examples below. One of the universal laws that one will find in the liquor act is "not serving or having minors on site of a liquor establishment." The age of drinking can range from 18-21 depending on where you live.

Canadian Laws that pertain to Bouncing

We can't stress the importance of knowing the general laws that pertain to this profession. Knowing your rights will keep you on the right side of the law and keep your actions justified. For example, if you have no idea what trespassing is or when you can legally escort someone off your property, you'll always be in a gray area when working the door. Read up on this stuff. **Knowledge is Power.**

Defense of a Person

Self-defense against unprovoked assault

34. (1) Everyone who is unlawfully assaulted without having provoked the assault is justified in repelling force by force if the force he uses is not intended to cause death or grievous bodily harm and is no more than is necessary to enable him to defend himself.

Extent of justification

(2) Every one who is unlawfully assaulted and who causes death or grievous bodily harm in repelling the assault is justified if
(a) He causes it under reasonable apprehension of death or grievous bodily harm from the violence with which the assault was originally made or with which the assailant pursues his purposes; and
(b) He believes, on reasonable grounds, that he cannot otherwise preserve himself from death or grievous bodily harm.
R.S., 1985, c. C-46, s. 34; 1992, c. 1, s. 60(F).

Self-defense in case of aggression

Anyone who has without justification assaulted another but did not commence the assault with intent to cause death or grievous bodily harm, or has without justification provoked an assault on himself by another, may justify the use of force subsequent to the assault if

(a) He uses the force

(i) Under reasonable apprehension of death or grievous bodily harm from the violence of the person whom he has assaulted or provoked, and

(ii) In the belief, on reasonable grounds, that it is necessary in order to preserve himself from death or grievous bodily harm;

(b) He did not, at any time before the necessity of preserving himself from death or grievous bodily harm arose, endeavor to cause death or grievous bodily harm; and

(c) He declined further conflict and quitted or retreated from it as far as it was feasible to do so before the necessity of preserving himself from death or grievous bodily harm arose.

R.S., c. C-34, s. 35.

Provocation

Provocation includes, for the purposes of sections 34 and 35, provocation by blows, words or gestures.

R.S., c. C-34, s. 36.

Preventing assault

37. (1) Every one is justified in using force to defend himself or any one under his protection from assault, if he uses no more force than is necessary to prevent the assault or the repetition of it.

Extent of justification

(2) Nothing in this section shall be deemed to justify the willful infliction of any hurt or mischief that is excessive, having regard to the nature of the assault that the force used was intended to prevent.

R.S., c. C-34, s. 37.

DEFENSE OF PROPERTY

Defense of personal property

38. (1) every one who is in peaceable possession of personal property, and every one lawfully assisting him, is justified

(a) In preventing a trespasser from taking it, or

(b) In taking it from a trespasser who has taken it,

If he does not strike or cause bodily harm to the trespasser.

Assault by trespasser

(2) Where a person who is in peaceable possession of personal property lays hands on it, a trespasser who persists in attempting to keep it or take it from him or from any one lawfully assisting him shall be deemed to commit an assault without justification or provocation. R.S., c. C-34, s. 38.

Defense with claim of right

39. (1) Every one who is in peaceable possession of personal property under a claim of right, and every one acting under his authority, is protected from criminal responsibility for defending that possession, even against a person entitled by law to possession of it, if he uses no more force than is necessary.

Defense without claim of right

(2) Every one who is in peaceable possession of personal property, but does not claim it as of right or does not act under the authority of a person who claims it as of right, is not justified or protected from criminal responsibility for defending his possession against a person who is entitled by law to possession of it.

R.S., c. C-34, s. 39.

Defense of dwelling

40. Every one who is in peaceable possession of a dwelling-house, and every one lawfully assisting him or acting under his authority, is justified in using as much force as is necessary to prevent any person from forcibly breaking into or forcibly entering the dwelling-house without lawful authority.

R.S., c. C-34, s. 40.

Defense of house or real property

41. (1) Every one who is in peaceable possession of a dwelling-house or real property, and every one lawfully assisting him or acting under his authority, is justified in using force to prevent any person from trespassing on the dwelling-house or real property, or to remove a trespasser there from, if he uses no more force than is necessary.

Assault by trespasser

(2) A trespasser who resists an attempt by a person who is in peaceable possession of a dwelling house or real property, or a person lawfully assisting him or acting under his authority to prevent his entry or to remove him, shall be deemed to commit an assault without justification or provocation.
R.S., c. C-34, s. 41.

Assertion of right to house or real property

42. (1) everyone is justified in peaceably entering a dwelling house or real property by day to take possession of it if he, or a person under whose authority he acts, is lawfully entitled to possession of it.

Assault in case of lawful entry

(2) Where a person

(a) Not having peaceable possession of a dwelling-house or real property under a claim of right, or

(b) Not acting under the authority of a person who has peaceable possession of a dwelling-house or real property under a claim of right, Assault's a person who is lawfully entitled to possession of it and who is entering it peaceably by day to take possession of it, for the purpose of preventing him from entering, the assault shall be deemed to be without justification or provocation.

Trespasser provoking assault

(3) Where a person

(a) Having peaceable possession of a dwelling-house or real property under a claim of right, or

(b) Acting under the authority of a person who has peaceable possession of a dwelling house or real property under a claim of right, Assault's any person who is lawfully entitled to possession of it and who is entering it peaceably by day to take possession of it, for the purpose of preventing him from entering, the assault shall be deemed to be provoked by the person who is entering.

R.S., c. C-34, s. 42.

MISCHIEF

Mischief

430. (1) every one commits mischief who willfully

(a) Destroys or damages property;

(b) Renders property dangerous, useless, inoperative or ineffective;

(c) Obstructs, interrupts or interferes with the lawful use, enjoyment or operation of property; or

(d) Obstructs, interrupts or interferes with any person in the lawful use, enjoyment or operation of property.

ASSAULT

Uttering threats

264.1 (1) every one commits an who, in any manner, knowingly utters, conveys or causes any person to receive a threat

(a) To cause death or bodily harm to any person;

(b) To burn, destroy or damage real or personal property; or

(c) To kill, poison or injure an animal or bird that is the property of any person.

Punishment

(2) Every one who commits an under paragraph (1)(a) is guilty of

(a) An indictable and liable to imprisonment for a term not exceeding five years; or

(b) An punishable on summary conviction and liable to imprisonment for a term not exceeding eighteen months.

Idem

(3) Every one who commits an under paragraph (1)(b) or (c)

(a) Is guilty of an indictable and liable to imprisonment for a term not exceeding two years; or

(b) Is guilty of an punishable on summary conviction.

R.S., 1985, c. 27 (1st Supp.), s. 38; 1994, c. 44, s. 16.

Assault

265. (1) A person commits an assault when

(a) Without the consent of another person, he applies force intentionally to that other person, directly or indirectly;

(b) He attempts or threatens, by an act or a gesture, to apply force to another person, if he has, or causes that other person to believe on reasonable grounds that he has, present ability to effect his purpose; or

(c) While openly wearing or carrying a weapon or an imitation thereof, he accosts or impedes another person or begs.

Application

(2) This section applies to all forms of assault, including sexual assault, sexual assault with a weapon, threats to a third party or causing bodily harm and aggravated sexual assault.

Consent

(3) For the purposes of this section, no consent is obtained where the complainant submits or does not resist by reason of

(a) The application of force to the complainant or to a person other than the complainant;

(b) Threats or fear of the application of force to the complainant or to a person other than the complainant;

(c) Fraud; or

(d) The exercise of authority.

Accuser's belief as to consent

(4) Where an accused alleges that he believed that the complainant consented to the conduct that is the subject-matter of the charge, a judge, if satisfied that there is sufficient evidence and that, if believed by the jury, the evidence would constitute a defense, shall instruct the jury, when reviewing all the evidence relating to the determination of the honesty of the accused belief, to consider the presence or absence of reasonable grounds for that belief.

R.S., c. C-34, s. 244; 1974-75-76, c. 93, s. 21; 1980-81-82-83, c. 125, s. 19.

Assault

266. Every one who commits an assault is guilty of

(a) An indictable offence and is liable to imprisonment for a term not exceeding five years; or

(b) An offence punishable on summary conviction.

R.S., c. C-34, s. 245; 1972, c. 13, s. 21; 1974-75-76, c. 93, s. 22; 1980-81-82-83, c. 125, s. 19.

Assault with a weapon or causing bodily harm

267. Every one who, in committing an assault,

(a) Carries, uses or threatens to use a weapon or an imitation thereof, or

(b) Causes bodily harm to the complainant,

Is guilty of an indictable offence and liable to imprisonment for a term not exceeding ten years or an offence punishable on summary conviction and liable to imprisonment for a term not exceeding eighteen months.

R.S., 1985, c. C-46, s. 267; 1994, c. 44, s. 17.

Aggravated assault

268. (1) Everyone commits an aggravated assault who wounds, maims, disfigures or endangers the life of the complainant.

Punishment

(2) Every one who commits an aggravated assault is guilty of an indictable offence and liable to imprisonment for a term not exceeding fourteen years.

Excision

(3) For greater certainty, in this section, "wounds" or "maims" includes to excise, infibulate or mutilate, in whole or in part, the labia majora, labia minora or clitoris of a person, except where

(a) A surgical procedure is performed, by a person duly qualified by provincial law to practice medicine, for the benefit of the physical health of the person or for the purpose of that person having normal reproductive functions or normal sexual appearance or function; or

(b) The person is at least eighteen years of age and there is no resulting bodily harm.

Consent

(4) For the purposes of this section and section 265, no consent to the excision, infibulation or mutilation, in whole or in part, of the labia majora, labia minora or clitoris of a person is valid, except in the cases described in paragraphs (3)(a) and (b).

R.S., 1985, c. C-46, s. 268; 1997, c. 16, s. 5.

Unlawfully causing bodily harm

269. Every one who unlawfully causes bodily harm to any person is guilty of

(a) An indictable offence and liable to imprisonment for a term not exceeding ten years; or

(b) An offence punishable on summary conviction and liable to imprisonment for a term not exceeding eighteen months.

Assaulting a peace officer

270. (1) Every one commits an offence who

(a) Assaults a public officer or peace officer engaged in the execution of his duty or a person acting in aid of such an officer;

(b) Assaults a person with intent to resist or prevent the lawful arrest or detention of himself or another person; or

(c) Assaults a person

(i) Who is engaged in the lawful execution of a process against lands or goods or in making a lawful distress or seizure, or

(ii) With intent to rescue anything taken under lawful process, distress or seizure.

Punishment

(2) Every one who commits an offence under subsection (1) is guilty of

(a) An indictable offence and is liable to imprisonment for a term not exceeding five years; or

(b) An offence punishable on summary conviction.

R.S., c. C-34, s. 246; 1972, c. 13, s. 22; 1980-81-82-83, c. 125, s. 19.

Disarming a peace officer

270.1 (1) Every one commits an offence who, without the consent of a peace officer, takes or attempts to take a weapon that is in the possession of the peace officer when the peace officer is engaged in the execution of his or her duty.

Definition of "weapon"

(2) For the purpose of subsection (1), "weapon" means any thing that is designed to be used to cause injury or death to, or to temporarily incapacitate, a person.

Punishment

(3) Every one who commits an offence under subsection (1) is guilty of

(a) An indictable offence and liable to imprisonment for a term of not more than five years; or

(b) An offence punishable on summary conviction and liable to imprisonment for a term of not more than eighteen months.
2002, c. 13, s. 11.

Sexual assault

271. (1) Every one who commits a sexual assault is guilty of

(a) An indictable offence and is liable to imprisonment for a term not exceeding ten years; or

(b) An offence punishable on summary conviction and liable to imprisonment for a term not exceeding eighteen months.

(2) [Repealed, R.S., 1985, c. 19 (3rd Supp.), s. 10]

R.S., 1985, c. C-46, s. 271; R.S., 1985, c. 19 (3rd Supp.), s. 10; 1994, c. 44, s. 19.

Sexual assault with a weapon, threats to a third party or causing bodily harm

272. (1) Every person commits an offence who, in committing a sexual assault,

(a) Carries, uses or threatens to use a weapon or an imitation of a weapon;

(b) Threatens to cause bodily harm to a person other than the complainant;

(c) Causes bodily harm to the complainant; or

(d) Is a party to the offence with any other person.

Punishment

(2) Every person who commits an offence under subsection (1) is guilty of an indictable offence and liable

(a) Where a firearm is used in the commission of the offence, to imprisonment for a term not exceeding fourteen years and to a minimum punishment of imprisonment for a term of four years; and

(b) In any other case, to imprisonment for a term not exceeding fourteen years.

R.S., 1985, c. C-46, s. 272; 1995, c. 39, s. 145.

Aggravated sexual assault

273. (1) Every one commits an aggravated sexual assault who, in committing a sexual assault, wounds, maims, disfigures or endangers the life of the complainant.

(2) Every person who commits an aggravated sexual assault is guilty of an indictable offence and liable

(a) Where a firearm is used in the commission of the offence, to imprisonment for life and to a minimum punishment of imprisonment for a term of four years; and

(b) In any other case, to imprisonment for life.

R.S., 1985, c. C-46, s. 273; 1995, c. 39, s. 146.

Meaning of "consent"

273.1 (1) Subject to subsection (2) and subsection 265(3), "consent" means, for the purposes of sections 271, 272 and 273, the voluntary agreement of the complainant to engage in the sexual activity in question.

Where no consent obtained

(2) No consent is obtained, for the purposes of sections 271, 272 and 273, where

(a) The agreement is expressed by the words or conduct of a person other than the complainant;

(b) The complainant is incapable of consenting to the activity;

(c) The accused induces the complainant to engage in the activity by abusing a position of trust, power or authority;

(d) The complainant expresses, by words or conduct, a lack of agreement to engage in the activity; or

(e) The complainant, having consented to engage in sexual activity, expresses, by words or conduct, a lack of agreement to continue to engage in the activity.

Subsection (2) not limiting

(3) Nothing in subsection (2) shall be construed as limiting the circumstances in which no consent is obtained.

1992, c. 38, s. 1.

Where belief in consent not a defense

273.2 It is not a defense to a charge under section 271, 272 or 273 that the accused believed that the complainant consented to the activity that forms the subject-matter of the charge, where

(a) The accused belief arose from the accused

(i) Self-induced intoxication, or

(ii) Recklessness or willful blindness; or

(b) The accused did not take reasonable steps, in the circumstances known to the accused at the time, to ascertain that the complainant was consenting.

1992, c. 38, s. 1.

Appendix

1. American Psychological Association

2. Greco-Roman Philosophic, Religious, and Voluntary Associations -Richard S. Ascoug

3. The Ladies; God Bless 'Em! - Shady Ladies of the Old West - Jeffords, Christine; private homepage at rootsweb.com

4. Snake-room (logging) (from Logger's Words of Yesteryears - Sorden, L.G.; Isabel J. Ebert; Madison, 1956, via wisconsinhistory.net)

5. Drinking in America: A History - Search for Consensus: Drinking and the War Against Pluralism, 1860-1920 - Lender, Mark Edward & Martin, James Kirby, The Free Press, New York, 1982

6. Schleswig, Iowa: The First 75 Years: Hohenzollern, Morgan Township: 1883-1899 - edited and compiled by Lillian M. (Kuehl) Jackson and Emma L. (Brasse) Struck, private homepage at rootsweb.com

7. Coney Island - Early History (1881 - 1903) (from private website westland.net)

8. When The Red Lights Went Out In San Diego - Macphail, Elizabeth, The Journal of San Diego History, Spring 1974, Volume 20,Number 2

9. Baltimore's Bawdy "Block" - Hull, Stephen; Stag, 1952

10. Wikipedia, the free encyclopedia

11. Monadnock Expandable Baton (MEB®)

12. The Crime Doctor – Chris McGoey

13. OCAT® training program

14. The Michigan Daily a student run newspaper serving the University of Michigan

15. Renaissance Swordsmanship: The Illustrated Use of Rapiers and Cut & Thrust Sword (Paladin Press, 1997) by John Clements

16. Tips to Help Spot Fraudulent IDs. Division of Police, Lexington, KY.

17. Forster JL, McGovern PG, Wagenaar AC, Wolfson M, Perry CL, Anstine PS. The ability of young people to purchase alcohol without age identification in northeastern Minnesota, USA. Addiction , 89:699-705, 1994.

18. Alan I. Leshner, Ph.D., Director, National Institute on Drug Abuse, National Institutes of Health

19. Preusser DF, Williams AF. Sales of alcohol to underage purchasers in three New York counties and Washington, D.C. Journal of Public Health Policy , 13: 306-317, 1992.

20. Schwartz RH, Farrow JA, Banks B, Giesel AE. Use of false ID cards and other deceptive methods to purchase alcoholic beverages during high school. Journal of the Addictive Diseases ,17(3):25-33, 1998.

21. Wagenaar AC, Toomey TL, Murray DM, Short BJ, Wolfson M, Jones-Webb R. Sources of alcohol for underage drinkers. Journal of Studies on Alcohol , 57(3):325-333, 1996.

22. The Hanford Fire Department operated by Fluor Hanford, Inc. for the

U.S. Department of Energy, Richland Operations Office. (Website)

23. The Austin Chronicle, 5/19/2006, The "One Percenters"

24. Outlaws MC website, What is a Outlaws MC 1%er Today

25. Bikernews.net

26. Missoulian, Storm Approaching

27. FBI Safe Street Violent Crime Initiative Report Fiscal Year 2000

28. Criminal Intelligence Service Canada (CISC) Annual Report

29. Five Hells Angels Motorcycle Gang Members and Associates Charged with Federal Racketeering Offenses

30. 12 Arrested in Raids Targeting a Methamphetamine and Cocaine Distribution Ring

31. CBC News, Five charged in biker gang killings

32. American Chronicle, Hell's Angels President, Sergeant-at-Arms Nailed on Drug Charges

33. Words from an MC patch holder

34. Las Vegas Review Journal, 4/30/2002; LAUGHLIN SHOOTOUT: Signs told of melee in making

35 The New York Times, 3/13/2002; Metro Briefing | New York: Central Islip: 73 Bikers Indicted

Lightning Source UK Ltd.
Milton Keynes UK
UKOW03f0951160215

246349UK00005B/299/P

9 781432 726416